IMPROV  'n' INK!

Overcoming…

"I Don't Know What to Write!"

IMPROV 'n' INK!™

Overcoming...

"I Don't Know What to Write!"

A Scaffolded Approach to Developing Writing Fluency Using Improvisation

A teacher's guide for ages nine-adult

Mary DeMichele

ACADEMIC PLAY

Publisher's Cataloging-In-Publication Data

DeMichele, Mary.
   Improv 'n ink : overcoming … "I don't know what to write" : a scaffolded approach to developing writing fluency using improvisation : a teacher's guide for ages nine-adult / Mary DeMichele ; illustrations by Wayne Logue. -- First edition.

   pages : illustrations ; cm

   Includes bibliographical references and index.
   ISBN-13: 978-0-9962613-0-2
   ISBN-10: 0-9962613-0-3

   1. Composition (Language arts) 2. English language--Rhetoric. 3. English language--Composition and exercises. 4. Improvisation in art. 5. Effective teaching. 6. Education--Experimental methods. 7. Creative writing. I. Logue, Wayne. II. Title. III. Title: Overcoming … "I don't know what to write" IV. Title: I don't know what to write

LB1576 .D46 2015
372.62/3   2015942954

Printed in the United States of America
First Edition

TABLE OF CONTENTS

PART 1

PART 2

PART 3

ACKNOWLEDGMENTS

First and foremost, I would like to thank my improv teacher, Bob Sapoff. From my years as a student in his class and as a performer in the professional troupe he directed, his consistent focus on the rule of "Yes, and…" was invaluable. His teaching of and unrelenting reminders to "Yes, and…" not only allowed for spontaneous and hilarious moments to erupt during performances, but also nurtured my personal and professional growth. Moreover, it eventually led to a deeper understanding of the transformative power of improv. Bob's continued guidance and support over the years enabled me to bring improv and all of its amazing and powerful benefits to others.

I would also like to extend a heartfelt thanks to Beth Baur, whose kind and supportive teaching style helped me build a firm foundation as an actor. This foundation transformed my teaching, enabling me to better understand the needs of my students and the effectiveness of "what worked and what didn't" in class; for that I am enormously grateful.

For their vision and commitment to finding ways to engage students and improve learning by embracing the integration of performing arts and academics, I would like to thank my former superintendent, Frank Gargiulo, and principal, Barbara Mendolla. I would also like to extend thanks to Mike Symczak for his assistance and support. I am also so fortunate to have worked with teachers and students throughout the country, whose enthusiasm and skepticism toward improv inspired and informed me.

I am grateful to my editor, Dr. Bob Burroughs, for his guidance and expertise in publishing, education, and language arts; and to Kathy Roberts for her detailed and instructive copyediting. I am deeply appreciative for the artistic talents of Amanda DeGraffenreid for her cover design and layout; and Wayne Logue, for his lively and fun illustrations.

I would like to thank Dr. Rich Allen for the wonderful opportunity to train with him and for his generosity in allowing me to share some of the facilitation strategies he has so effectively articulated in his trainings and books. I would also like to thank Fran Zidron, who taught me how to organize my intuitive teaching within an instructional design framework.

I am most grateful to my Mom, a master teacher, whose endless encouragement, support, and belief in my ability to write has helped me persevere in the completion of this book. I must credit my Dad for igniting my interest in the arts. For the wonderful time spent watching performances from Baryshnikov to the *Black Adder*, and all the *Monty Pythons* in between, thanks, Dad.

My husband's support and encouragement cannot be understated. From his occasional edits to his challenge to explain improv as a process, I am immensely thankful.

INTRODUCTION

IMPROV DEVELOPS WRITING?

Yes, those 3- to 5-minute improv games with often hilarious outcomes can help students develop their writing fluency. Research shows that students who are reluctant, resistant, or just find themselves occasionally frustrated are able to increase the length of their individual writing after following this short sequence of scaffolded improv games and improv writing activities (DeMichele, 2015). The reason for a student's reluctance to write is not always evident to the teacher, and could be rooted in a deficit of literacy skills and/or social-emotional skills. Improv provides an effective and efficient intervention to address both simultaneously. With 90% of the time in collaborative groups and 70% of that time engaged in oral games, students progress rapidly through a series of essential literacy skills that impact the ability to write, while concurrently nurturing the development of important social-emotional skills that also affect a students' individual writing. Such a counterintuitive approach was not conceived in theory, but was instead discovered organically. It was the students themselves who had independently transferred specific improv concepts and skills to their writing.

The discovery of this connection would lead me to researching the impact and role of improv on writing fluency and ultimately to the writing of this book. My experience of using improv in the classroom, however, began before this finding and would significantly influence the book's direction and format. The next few pages reveal why the focus of *Improv 'n Ink* extends beyond *what* literacy skills improv can develop, and instead gives extensive attention to *how* and *why* improv increases writing fluency.

IMPROV IN MY CLASSROOM

Like so many others, I discovered improv in adulthood and quickly realized that practicing improv had a profound and transformative effect on my professional and personal life. I had the wonderful opportunity to be a founding member of an improv troupe and for years mustered enough energy after work to perform with amazing individuals in and around New Jersey and New York City. Being a high school teacher, I thought how wonderful it would be to share improv with my students, so I introduced improv games into my classroom.

Students developed interpersonal skills, communication skills, and social-emotional skills. They were engaged, energetic, and eager to participate. Like any teacher, I had anecdotes to share: awesome stories of student success, breakthroughs, and the creation of positive, inclusive, and supportive relationships throughout entire classes. These stories were often met with polite but seemingly dismissive smiles. Even the decades of available research supporting the use of dramatic arts in the classrooms and evidence that drama and improv could improve motivation, self-esteem, engagement, communication skills, etc., were greeted with polite but dismissive smiles. Why were other educators not excited about a tool they could use to help engage and meet the educational needs of their students? Why were they not interested in wanting to know how to use improv? Although I was disappointed and confused by this seeming disinterest, I continued using improv and sharing anecdotes. This complacent frustration of being content that my students were benefiting, but unsatisfied because I could not interest others, changed one day after school.

SHOUTING FROM THE ROOFTOP

Zach was a nice kid who had enormous energy. I knew through teachers' stories that he could be an absolute annoyance in the classroom for teachers and even for students. He was the type of kid who would be described as "bouncing off the walls." In the spring of his senior year, he was cast in a play I was directing. Due to scheduling conflicts we had not done a complete run-through of the play with all of the scenes in consecutive order or with all the student actors in attendance until one day before the performance. This run-through was the first time Zach had even seen many scenes of the play. After we had done our first run-through of a 90-minute play, which was pretty exhausting, I told all the kids to relax for a bit. They all collapsed; that is, except for Zach. Instead he jumped up and acted the entire play by himself in 15 minutes. He acted each part, with actual dialogue from the script. The lines he said actually were important and pivotal lines that moved the story forward. He did improvise some dialogue, but also knew the other actors' lines. He even acted each character as the other students had developed them. He used their gestures, their expressions, their timing, and their intonation of delivery. Zach did it all, brilliantly.

His peers were surprised and entertained. I was astonished at what I was witnessing. I sent kids out to bring in other teachers and administrators to witness this, but it was after school and people had left or were in meetings. I wanted to shout from the rooftop of the school with joy and amazement of what I had seen this kid do, but also with utter frustration and sadness that these abilities may not have always been honored, explored or known about during his education. When those 15 minutes were over and Zach beamed in accomplishment and his peers cheered wildly, I had only a story to tell. An amazing and informative story, but one that would be acknowledged only with the polite, dismissive smiles.

I decided I had to move beyond sharing stories. All teachers have stories. We all do and we all share them. I needed to do something different. I was going to collect evidence. Maybe then others could see that drama and improv really worked beyond reaching a few kids and just being fun. Maybe they would realize they could use it in their classroom and their students could share in the benefits, developing skills they could use in school and in life. I kept a journal and conducted surveys, compiling personal statements and statistical information of how the students felt about the games, the skills they thought they had gained, and if they felt their schoolwork had been affected.

WRITING WITH "YES, AND..."

At one point I realized that students had independently transferred the use of the improv rule *"Yes, and...,"* which prompts the player to accept another's offer and build upon it, to their writing. This was apparent by their willingness to write, the increase in the length of their writing, and that when questioned about these changes they said "Yes, and..." was helping them write. When opportunities arose, I conducted research to see if a scaffolded sequence of improv games and improv writing activities could help students increase the length of their writing. The results were exciting. Whether the students participated in classes over six days or six weeks, regular education students showed a 50% increase in the length of their writing, and special needs and "at risk" students showed a

100-300% increase over the comparison group or time period (DeMichele, 2015). Since writing is an essential skill in most if not all classes, and almost everyone has an issue with "thinking of what else to write" at some time, I thought these results would create real interest in improv. Teachers would now not only accept that improv was an impactful intervention, but would want to use it themselves.

THINKING WITH "YES, BUT…"

My immediate reaction was to share what I had learned with others. It quickly became apparent that convincing others to incorporate improv into their classes would require more than my enthusiasm, anecdotes of student success, surveys, and even numerical data. When I had shared my anecdotes of improv's impact in the class, teachers did not further the discussion about improv, but instead shared their own stories about their students. When I began to present the evidence I had gathered, then others began to voice reasons for their lack of interest in using improv. Those polite smiles were actually dismissive, not so much because they didn't accept the evidence, but because of unfamiliarity with improv and misconceptions about what it was and how it worked.

Some could not see beyond the "fun" of the games and understand improv's ability to rapidly develop educational skills. Some would try, but would not be successful due to how they facilitated the games. Others were just not interested because they didn't believe it was something they could ever do or would even work for "their" students. Most generally accepted that improv could be useful in the classroom, but the misconceptions about improv thwarted any further curiosity or intention to use it. They had been exposed to all the claims of what improv could do. What they lacked was an understanding of *how* and *why* it actually worked to produce literacy, social-emotional and performance skills.

ADDRESSING COMMON MISCONCEPTIONS

Misconceptions about improv are often voiced after an individual has been presented with evidence that it works. Even if the individual receives the type of evidence they value most, whether it be qualitative or quantitative; and even if the data is earth-shatteringly conclusive, they will have misconceptions. A simple denial of "Yes, but…" will be uttered or inferred. "Yes, that sounds great, but it just wouldn't work in my class because…". Misconceptions are due to their unfamiliarity with improv or because of an experience with improv that was poorly or incorrectly facilitated. So even after they accept the evidence, these misconceptions will inhibit them from moving forward and using improv to improve writing fluency or any of the other literacy, social-emotional, or performance-based skills it develops. Below are some common misconceptions voiced by educators and how this book addresses them.

"Improv Games are Just for Fun Breaks."

When an improv game is played on occasion or without its foundational rules and structures, then it only serves as a fun activity filling a few moments of time. When the games are introduced with structure and sequence, they can be fun and they are also powerful! Improv is capable of supporting social-emotional, academic, and literacy skills. It engages and motivates students of diverse abilities, backgrounds, and educational needs. *Chapters 2* through *4* offer detailed explanations, insights, and research on how and why improv can serve as a powerful educational intervention and pedagogy.

"Improv is Chaotic."

No. Improv is a process with specific rules and structures that must be followed in order for the games to work successfully. It is through the consistent practice of these rules and structures that spontaneity can exist. It is these same rules and structures that will develop and support literacy skills, positively impact behavior management, and advance interpersonal, social-emotional, and collaborative skills. *Chapter 2* introduces improv as a process, and *Chapter 3* describes the role of improv's rules and structures.

"I Already Use Games and Group Work."

Improv games are different from other group activities or cooperative learning groups, because improv is collaborative. The skills students develop working collaboratively transform the educational experience for the individual and for the class as a whole. Group work often follows a form of cooperative learning, which differs from collaboration as students tend to have specific roles as they complete a defined task. In collaborative groups, students participate as equals co-creating a project. The collaborative nature of improv games is supported and structured by the rule of "Yes, and…". When games are implemented without an understanding of "Yes, and…," they serve as an activity that students engage in for that moment. When "Yes, and…" is added, a spirit of collaboration, creativity, confidence, and emotional safety grows, not only for that instructional moment, but for the duration of the class and school year, benefiting the individual student and the class. *Chapter 3* offers further explanation on the difference between cooperative groups and collaborative groups, and how improv is based upon collaboration and offers consistent practice and development of collaborative skills.

"Improv is Great for Social Skills, but I Have Content to Cover."

Improv is generally accepted as an effective means of helping students develop confidence, social-emotional skills, and interpersonal skills. Although teachers understand that these skills are essential to a student's ability to learn and ultimate success, with so much content to cover they sometimes view a student's social and personal growth as important, but ultimately someone else's responsibility. Teachers can use improv to deepen the learning of their content while simultaneously developing personal and social skills with no extra effort. If content is integrated into an improv game and the game is facilitated with respect to its rules, then the desired social-emotional skills will develop. This in turn creates a mind-set and learning environment that will further support the learning of content throughout the year. *Chapter 3* explains how one rule, "Yes, and…" and a four-step improv structure enables all skills to develop simultaneously. The Game Plans in *Chapters 6 and 7* offer ideas on how content can be integrated into improv structures.

"I Just Don't Have Time for Another Instructional Approach."

This book was developed with respect and consideration to the amount of content, curricular standards, and standardized assessments for which teachers are responsible. Teachers may choose to implement the games devoting only a few minutes or as much time that is available. In as few as five lessons, gains in student engagement, individual and group motivation, and skill development will take root. Although this book is quite detailed in order to create a firm understanding of how improv works, actual facilitation and performance is not complex with each game only 3 to 5 minutes in length and corresponding writing activities only 5 to 10 minutes. Once learned, games and concepts can be integrated with class curricular content and be seamlessly embedded into daily instruction.

"I Don't Want My Students to Think They Are Not in Class."

Agreed! Language and techniques used throughout this book are chosen to help the students remember they are in an instructional setting. I am a firm believer in play as an essential part of learning and although research, educators, and science support its role, "play" and "games" can still seem frivolous, as well as create the fear that students will see them as separate from curricular objectives and expectations. Words that might create the sense of another environment, for example the terms actor, director, and stage, are not used for instructional purposes. The word game is used throughout the book because the activities are borrowed from improvisational theater, which calls them games. Feel free to refer to them as activities instead if that will help students understand them as part of class instruction.

"There is Just Not Enough Room."

The *Improv 'n Ink* sequence of games is designed for the classroom, not for the stage. No game presented necessitates the removal of furniture. In fact, all of the games in the *Improv 'n Ink* sequence can be done with students standing in front of the class and seated at their desks in groups. Seating and standing arrangement suggestions are given in each Game Plan in *Part 2* of this book.

"I'm Not Comfortable with Students Moving Around the Room."

That is understandable. The five core games of the sequence do not require any free movement or physical contact. Expressive movement, such as physical gestures, in the five core games is optional or contained, occurring with no physical contact or movement around the room. Games that are movement and/or scene based are contained in the Additional Game Section (*Chapter 7)*, and are optional, but recommended when the teacher and students are comfortable.

"Isn't Playing Games Too Childish on the Secondary or Adult level?"

No. These games are improv games played from the elementary level to higher education and beyond. In higher education, improvisational games are being used to train first-year medical students and students in MBA programs (Berk & Trieber 2009). Corporations, doctors, and lawyers frequently hire improvisational trainers and play some of these very same games in order to help them function better as a team, find creative solutions, and develop better social and work-related skills. Improv will play a role in how we prepare our students and workforce for the innovative economy in which we now live (Sawyer, 2006). *Chapter 2* discusses improv's return to the classroom.

"But I'm Just Not the Dramatic Type."

This book presents improv in a friendly and manageable way. There are no costume or prop requirements. The teacher does not need to dress up or read with dramatic flair. They do not need to be familiar with the techniques of staging until they introduce scene-based games in the Additional Game section in *Chapter 7*. They do not need to be improvisers, actors, or extroverts in any way. Each game and writing activity is prepared in a lesson-plan format with notes and examples to aid teachers with or without a background in drama or improv. *Chapter 1* details why the games are much less threatening than other more complex improv games.

"Some Students are Shy."

Within the world of improv there are many wonderful and exciting games; however, some of those games can be intimidating to individuals who may not be extroverts or feel secure performing in front of their peers. The games selected for this program were specifically chosen and designed to be the least threatening for students and teachers. *Chapter 1* explains how the games chosen create much less threat than more complex improv games. The design and sequence of the games immediately promotes a spirit of respect and collaboration, thus creating an emotionally safe environment for the students in which to develop the targeted skills.

WHY I WROTE THIS BOOK

My experiences taught me that using improv and helping others understand and enjoy the power of improv in their classroom involved more than just being excited about and familiar with the games. In order for improv to be an effective and efficient classroom intervention, it is necessary for an instructor to be able to facilitate it and then articulate how and why it worked. Furthermore, an instructor should be able to replicate the results to achieve the support from administration so its use can be sustained over time and perhaps adopted by others. Other books that offer improv for the classroom may discuss what improv is and what it can do. This book goes further, exploring and explaining how and why improv is such an amazing and impactful educational intervention. In order for improv to be used to increase writing fluency, teachers must understand how it works, facilitate it correctly, and integrate it into classroom practices. With this in mind, this book was written in great detail, sharing insight, experience, and research to help teachers:

Articulate not just what improv games can do, but also how and why they so effectively and efficiently produce desired skills and results. A teacher may realize that improv is an amazingly effective intervention, but if they are unable to explain to others how and why it works, it might be simply dismissed as something not replicable. The gains made by students may be credited to the teacher or students being just "good" or because improv is just "fun." Understanding and articulating how improv produces fluency and other essential skills will dispel misconceptions about how it works, thus encouraging others to try it and practice it correctly.

▶ *Chapter 2* presents improv's role in the classroom.

▶ *Chapters 2 and 3* explores how improv increases engagement and motivation, deepens learning, and develops valuable skills.

▸ *Chapter 4* discusses and presents research on how improv and the *Improv 'n Ink* sequence develops writing fluency.

Facilitate the games and writing activities with clear understanding and respect for the rules and structures, so that skill development will be achieved and motivation increased. The relativity small but select group of games presented will help develop a foundational understanding of improv for both teachers and students. Taking the time to learn and appreciate improv will enable the teacher to successfully and comfortably teach improv for their purposes: integrating it to enrich content, improve performance and class culture, and to meet standards.

▸ *Chapter 5* offers strategies and information on how to teach and facilitate the games.

▸ *Chapters 6 and 7* present the sequenced and additional games, complete with examples, directions, and ideas for integration, as well as additional notes and information.

Replicate positive results by understanding and respecting improv as a process and realizing that results can be quantified. In order for improv to have a sustained presence within a class, school, or district, it is essential for decisionmakers to understand that the growth experienced by one group of students can be replicated with other classes. It is vital that improv be understood and respected not only as an art, but also as a replicable process capable of producing the desired educational outcomes.

▸ *Chapters 2 and 3* discuss improv as a process, composed of both rules and structures.

▸ *Chapter 3* details how improv's rules and structures impact skill development, motivation, learning, and engagement.

▸ *Chapter 4* explores how and why improv and the specific sequence of games in this book develop writing fluency.

Sustain improv as an educational intervention through the adaptation of improv concepts and structures into classroom practices, and by the integration of course content into improv structures. It is common in schools to adopt an intervention, find that it works, and then just abandon it for the next newer approach. This is obviously a huge waste of time and money, and beyond frustrating for teachers who are successfully using that intervention. In order to help sustain the presence of improv, the rules and structures of improv need to be integrated and adapted to other classroom practices and content areas. This will help students transfer skills learned through improv to their other coursework. When improv is sustained as a classroom practice, improv's ability to develop skills as well as motivate, engage, and deepen learning will continue, positively transforming the individual as well as the culture of the class.

▸ *Chapters 6 and 7* include ideas on how to integrate improv's rules and structures into classroom practices and course content.

BOOK OVERVIEW

Improv 'n Ink presents a structured, evidence-based approach using improv to help the reluctant writer develop writing fluency. Using a scaffolded sequence of specific improv storytelling games with corresponding collaborative and individual writing activities, students develop a way of thinking that will enable them to present their thoughts with coherence and flow. In as few as five

lessons, this sequence helps students address social-emotional and literacy deficits that may be impeding their ability to put their thoughts on paper. With students increasing the length of their writing, teachers can proceed to teach the writing process or assess content knowledge.

In addition to developing writing fluency, the *Improv 'n Ink* sequence presents an inclusive and dynamic way to teach narrative writing and develop other literacy skills such as speaking, listening, reading fluency, and reading comprehension. Social-emotional skills, including collaboration, self-esteem, and respect are simultaneously developed along with performance skills such as creativity, adaptability, and spontaneity. With its 3- to 5-minute game structures and inherent ability to reach and engage students of diverse educational needs, learning modalities, generations, and backgrounds, improv is a valuable instructional intervention fitting easily into the already content packed classroom.

The scaffolding of both literacy and improv skills through the sequencing of specific games helps both the teacher and student implement improv comfortably and with confidence. The format of this three-part manual enables the teacher to access the information they need quickly.

➢ Grounded in research, *Part 1* helps teachers understand improv's impact on writing fluency and learning. With this understanding they are better prepared to successfully facilitate the games and articulate to others how and why the *Improv 'n Ink* sequence works.

➢ Detailed instructions for each game and activity are given in *Part 2* so that individuals with no experience facilitating or participating in improv can feel confident and comfortable. Each game includes overview, example, new terms, directions, coaching and notes, rubrics, and how to integrate with classroom practices and content.

➢ *Part 3* offers supplemental materials.

➢ There is no *glossary* contained in this book. All relevant improv terms are contained within the game in which they are introduced. This is done for the convenience of the teacher so they do not have to repeatedly flip through the book while they gain an understanding of the game and how to facilitate it. Terms are listed in the *index*.

This scaffolded and sequenced approach enables teachers to articulate how and why improv works, replicate positive results and sustain improv as a recognized classroom strategy so that students may develop their writing fluency, overcoming, *"I don't know what to write!"*

PART 1

*

HOW & WHY IMPROV DEVELOPS WRITING FLUENCY

*

1

IMPROV AND THE RELUCTANT WRITER:

Writing with "Yes, and..."

It is a typical day. The bell rings. Students bustle into the classroom eventually taking their seats. The teacher says, "Take out your notebooks. You have ten minutes to write about…" and gives a topic. About seven minutes pass and the teacher announces, "You still have about three more minutes to write," and then walks around to check on their progress. To the teacher's dismay, there are quite a few blank papers and papers with much less writing than one would have expected for the amount of time given. And then the frustrating exchanges begin:

Teacher:	Why is this paper blank?
Student A:	I don't know what to write.
Teacher:	Only three sentences? You've had almost 10 minutes to write.
Student B:	I don't know what else to write.
Teacher:	Is that it?
Student C:	I'm done.
Teacher:	Well, that's not enough. Write more.

A RELUCTANCE TO WRITE

Sound familiar? The ability to write is required in both the educational and professional worlds, and yet everyone at some point suffers from not being able to think of what to write or what else to write. Students who are momentarily or persistently resistant to writing can be a formidable, frustrating, and potentially costly situation for any teacher or student. One might feel only temporarily resistant or unfocused; or one may have become consistently resistant to writing assignments. Many students have stopped trying to write by the time they have reached high school, if not before.

WRITING, WRITING EVERYWHERE

With standardized tests demanding well-written and structured writing samples from students, the scenario given can be quite frustrating and costly for teachers. Writing across the curriculum has been embraced and practiced for decades; and now with open-ended questions being included as part of standardized tests including math, all subject area teachers need students to be able to write. Students must produce enough writing so that teachers can address any deficiencies, teach mechanics, form and structure, content material, and assess skill or content mastery.

Although language arts teachers are responsible for teaching writing, teachers in other areas do not always have the luxury of waiting and hoping that their students will gain a proficiency level and desire to write in language arts class and then transfer those skills to their class. First, language arts teachers may not be focused on the topic of writing when other teachers need their students to write. Second, if the school is using a half-year block schedule, the student may not even have language arts when they need to write in other classes. Last, students sometimes resist writing at all or to their fullest potential because they are "not in English class." In some cases those students don't write in English class either, but the disconnect when it comes to transferring writing skills to other classes is common.

Throughout schools, language arts teachers expend great focus and effort to teaching and guiding students through the writing process: prewriting, drafting, revising, editing, and publishing. This entire endeavor is thwarted if a student will not pick up a pen or does not produce a long enough draft to even warrant revising. So that students can continue experiencing and practicing the entire writing process, teachers often turn to additional strategies.

COMMON INTERVENTIONS

Two common approaches used by teachers to increase a student's willingness to write are external prompting and attempting to engage students in fun or high-interest topics. Although these may be effective for a given writing assignment, the students do not necessarily transfer their prompted fluency or interest to future assignments. These approaches, although common, fail to address why a student is resistant to writing.

EXTERNAL PROMPTING

External prompting is used to help students produce a longer writing sample. Although a common and sometimes effective intervention, it can prove exhausting for the teacher, cause classroom management issues, increase student resistance, and produce only momentary gains. With external prompting, the teacher asks guiding questions, permitting the student to write the answer to each question. For example, if the topic was, "What did you do on your day off from school?" The teacher might ask, "What time did you wake up?" "Did you have breakfast?" "What did you have?" "What did you do after breakfast?"

This external prompting proves somewhat effective for the student with that particular assignment, but lacks in producing lasting results. The student learns to rely on the teacher for prompting each time there is an assignment. This learned helplessness inhibits the student from gaining confidence in their ability to freely and comfortably engage in writing. It also proves quite ineffective in terms of time and classroom management. Often a teacher is faced with more than one student who needs individual prompting. The other students in need of individual attention must therefore wait for help and are consequently delayed in starting the assignment. They instead watch, wait, and maybe disrupt, while other students begin and finish. As a result, those students left waiting often grow resentful and resistant to future writing assignments. There is also the risk that external prompting may create an isolating environment for those students who depend on being prompted thought by thought. They will sometimes feel "stupid" and singled out in front of their peers and may begin to resist writing assignments to avoid feeling humiliation or embarrassment.

HIGH-INTEREST TOPICS

Another common strategy used to encourage disengaged students to produce writing is to present high-interest or fun topics. Some students may be engaged by the humor of an assignment or their passion for a topic, forgetting anxieties that regularly impede them. This approach may prove effective for a single assignment, but often fails to motivate disengaged students to produce writing on a consistent basis. A student who has never figured out how to build from one thought to the next or gained the confidence to accept their ideas as being worthy enough to put on paper for themselves and others to review may remain resistant when future assignments are not of high interest or are accompanied by external prompting.

ENTER...IMPROV

I, too, tried to "help" my students by prompting them so they would put their thoughts down on paper; however, I was run ragged trying to help student after student. It became apparent that even if they grasped the writing elements that were taught during the previous assignment, there they would sit with a blank paper unable to begin. I assigned some high-interest topics, in hopes that a fervor for writing would be ignited, but increases in a student's length of writing just didn't translate to the less personally interesting topics. To my surprise, improv changed all of this. I began to introduce my classes to some of the games and rules in the hopes that both instruction and student achievement would be positively impacted. The results of integrating improv games and concepts, such as *"Yes and…"* in the classroom were amazing.

"Yes, and…" is the foundational rule of improv. This simple but powerful phrase prompts the player to acknowledge the idea another player offers and then build upon it. Through the consistent practice of "Yes, and…" individuals learn to suspend their judgment of themselves and of others. Each new offer will take an idea or scene into a new, unscripted, spontaneous direction. "Yes, and…" allows storylines to move forward and the ensemble to contribute and create in collaboration. This dynamic concept of "Yes and…," when understood and embraced, helps one to work collaboratively, connect and grow their own thoughts and ideas, gain confidence, learn presentation skills, develop creativity and spontaneity, and so much more that will be discussed throughout the book.

By introducing improv into my classes, cooperative and collaborative groups became more effective. Students felt more comfortable and confident participating or sharing their thoughts. All of their ideas mattered. Students contributed without fearing they would be rejected, laughed at, dismissed, or disregarded. Students began to engage in class activities comfortably and eagerly.

Previously disengaged students became enthusiastic students in class discussions and content reviews. Tolerance, respect, and understanding between students blossomed as the concepts of improv nurtured a sense of collaboration and cohesiveness within the class. Through the integration of these concepts and skills, interpersonal and communication skills developed fostering an overall class environment conducive to learning. Behavior management issues of individual students began to disappear as those individuals modified and regulated their own behavior. Students gained an amazing sense of empowerment over their learning experience.

Most of those results I had hoped for and expected. What really got my attention and piqued my curiosity was what happened when the students started applying the concept of *"Yes, and..."* in a way I had not anticipated. They had transferred it to their writing assignments. Those statements of, "I don't know what to write," "I don't have anything else to write about," and "I'm done," began to disappear. Improv was impacting writing fluency.

IMPROV AND WRITING FLUENCY

A student's reluctance to write may be due to social-emotional reasons or literacy-based deficits. With individual reasons usually not known to the teacher, improv serves as an effective broad-based instructional intervention. Improv provides a framework that takes students rapidly through essential literacy processes seen on the emergent level. When students participate in this scaffolded sequence of improv games and improv writing activities, they are exposed to and practice these processes addressing deficits in social-emotional and literacy skills important to writing. *Chapter 4* discusses in detail how the *Improv 'n Ink* sequence accomplishes this.

THE IMPROV 'N INK GAMES

Although there are many wonderful resources available that offer large selections of improv games *Improv 'n Ink* instead, offers a carefully selected and sequenced group of improv games for the purpose of building writing fluency. The five core games are presented in a powerful and effective sequence, allowing the teacher and the students to achieve maximum results with a fairly minimal amount of time invested. The *Improv 'n Ink* sequence of games presented in this book are scaffolded to not only facilitate the learning of improv, but also to enable the students to move from collaborative speech to individual writing. Three of the five essential improv games have corresponding writing activities. Additional games that are movement and/or scene based are offered and can be integrated into the five-game sequence after students and teachers are comfortable with the basic structure and rules of improv. In order to ensure success of implementation, detailed game plans are presented and include instructions, new terminology, examples, teacher's notes, a corresponding rubric, and ideas for how the game structure can be adapted to deepen specific content knowledge and classroom practices. A brief description of the games and writing activities follows. More detailed information regarding the games and how to facilitate them is contained in the *Chapters 5, 6 and 7*.

MOST FRIENDLY/LEAST THREATENING

These games were specifically chosen because at a minimum they only require teachers and students to perform two actions that are familiar and practiced every day at school. The students must face forward and simply speak loud enough to be heard. This allows them to comfortably focus on the improv concepts that are presented and reinforced in the scaffolded sequence. Movement is not required in any of these games; however, students are allowed to make physical gestures and act out what they are saying while standing or sitting in place. The following additional notes pinpoint details that make the improv games used in the *Improv 'n Ink* sequence less threatening than other common improv games.

► These games are noncompetitive. Students need not fear being eliminated by being called "out," which would limit their opportunity to develop the intended skills. If a student worried they might be eliminated through competition they might become anxious or perceive fellow students as a threat (Spolin, 1999). This would strip the spirit of collaboration from the class and consequently much of the benefits of this approach.

► In most games, students work and perform in small peer groups. In some games, all students participate simultaneously, thus eliminating an audience. Teachers should allow students to create their own groups initially. After they become comfortable with the concepts and the class develops cohesiveness–making it more emotionally safe–grouping should be more random.

► Some students feel "silly" or "embarrassed" if required to do movement in front of others and will consequently become resistant. Within the five core games, movement is optional. Students may add dramatic movement without moving from their designated spot if they choose. This allowance of choice will foster positive student involvement. Some students will choose to move because it is how they best process information. Their movement in these games will in no way detract from the experience of the other students. The games offered in the Additional Game section are movement-based and can be integrated into the core sequence at an appropriate time.

YES, AND-PLANNING

There are many "Yes, and..." games. Yes, And-Planning, was chosen because students are generally comfortable and familiar with brainstorming or planning something in class. The rule of *"Yes, and..."* offers a new structure to a familiar activity. This allows them to focus on *"Yes, and..."* and giving and taking attention from each other. The game, Yes, And-Planning starts with a group of three and can later be expanded to include every member of the class. Guided by such a simple phrase, this game is a powerful and efficient activity to introduce a spirit and understanding of collaboration. The game may look and sound something like this:

Three students stand or sit facing the class.

Teacher:	*(speaking to the class)* What would you like these three people to plan?
Audience/Class:	A car!
Student A:	Let's plan a car.
Student B:	Yes, and the car can be red.
Student C:	Yes, and it can have flames on it.
Student B:	Yes, and they can be real flames.

Student C:	Yes, and it can have an amazing sound system.
Student A:	Yes, and the sound system can be synced with the flames.
Student B:	Yes, and it can go from 0-300 in 60 seconds.
Student C:	Yes, and it can fly.
Student A:	Yes, and it can run on solar power.

STORYTELLING GAMES

Not all Storytelling Games are Improv Storytelling Games

Many of the storytelling games offered in this book might be familiar as they are sometimes used as fun games in and out of the classroom. If the games, however, are not played with respect to the rules and structures of improv, they will merely serve as a fun break and will not develop writing fluency, as well as the other essential language arts, social-emotional, and performance skills that improv supports. Only with a respect and understanding of the rules and structures will the skills be developed in a timely manner.

One-Word Storytelling Games

Unlike many other improv games, the one-word storytelling games are somewhat of an equalizer of abilities at all age levels. In many improv games, individuals with certain strengths will immediately excel, leaving those without those abilities on the sidelines and feeling a bit anxious. In the one-word storytelling games, the individuals who are perhaps more verbally comfortable will actually struggle a bit, as they are confined to only one-word and must listen for and accept the word offered by the others. Having to only offer one-word, individuals with a lesser verbal ability or level of comfort will feel on par with the other students. All students learn very quickly that they must listen, react, adapt, share control, and co-create. These games immediately produce a higher level of comfort and participation than many other improv games. Important: Students who are English language learners may find these one-word story games frustrating, as they are probably still mastering tense, syntax, and other aspects of the language. The frustration will be felt by the ELL students as they try to offer a word that makes sense at that point in the sentence, as well as by the group members who have to continue the sentence.

Phrase and Sentence Story Games

The Story-Story structure, which allows for students to offer phrases and sentences, can easily maintain a sense of inclusiveness and accomplishment as the teacher directs how much the individual is expected to offer and no one is eliminated. These games also introduce genre/story-style to the students. The two story-games in the sequence that allow for offers of phrases and sentences will prove easier for English Language Learners (ELL) as they will be able to convey to others what they mean, even if it is not grammatically correct. Allowing the student to finish their sentence, then having a new narrator begin a new sentence will eliminate fluency issues.

STORY WRITING GAMES

Many teachers who have used storytelling games will instruct their students to play the game and then sit down and write the story they created orally. While this approach will serve auditory learners and engage recall skills, it may not help students transition from oral fluency to writing fluency. The collaborative writing activities in this book follow the structure of the corresponding oral improv game, but instead of the students participating orally, they collaboratively write the stories. This step allows for students to transfer essential literacy skills gained during collaborative oral games to collaborative written games. After having participated in the collaborative improv game orally and in writing, the student will have the opportunity to write their own individual story, thus allowing the trust and fluency gained during collaborative activities to transfer to their individual writing.

Example: We Are... (one-word story)

Student A	Student B	Action *(optional)*
We...	are...	Students stand facing audience.
walking...	through...	Students begin walking in place, still facing the audience.
the...	desert.	
Suddenly,...	a...	
ferocious...	giant...	
scorpion...	attacks.	Students stop walking and show a giant scorpion attacking.
We...	throw...	
sand...	and...	Students show themselves throwing sand...
cactuses.	The...	and cacti.
scorpion...	cries...	.
whwaaa...	and...	
goes...	home.	
We...	go...	
home...	too.	Student show themselves going home, still in place.
The...	End.	

Example: Story- Story (phrase and sentence story game)

A group of perhaps seven students stand in a line facing the class. There is no required movement in this game. A student may gesture or move slightly acting out their portion of the story as they tell it. The teacher stands in front of the line, but not to block the audience's view. The seven players all watch the teacher. The teacher directs this story by pointing at a student. The student must tell a portion of the story until the teacher points at another student. The teacher continues to direct different students to tell the story. This process will continue as students establish CROW (character, relationship, objective, and where) and create a problem (conflict). Finally, the teacher directs a student to solve the problem (resolving the conflict and ending the story).

Teacher:	What kind of story would you like these people to tell?
Class:	Action Adventure

Student A:	The professor went in search of the lost treasure.
Student C:	A chest of gold was hidden by the…
Student E:	meanest pirate ever, Plaid Beard. He hid it on a deserted island.
Student B:	The professor got on his boat and went to the island. There he found…
Student F:	a message in a bottle. It was the lost map. He followed it to the…
Student A:	volcano. He climbed it but when he got to the top he fell in and…
Student D:	saw the treasure as he was falling. He grabbed a ledge and pulled himself onto it.
Student G:	He attached a drone to it and flew himself and the treasure out of the volcano.
Student C:	Then the curse made the volcano erupt.
Teacher:	End it.
Student F:	The professor and the treasure were thrown back in the boat. He sailed home very rich. The End.

ADDITIONAL IMPROV GAMES

Improv games that require movement or are scene-based and thus more complex to facilitate and perform are offered separate from this sequence. These games can be integrated into the core sequence when the teacher is comfortable. These games will offer the more kinesthetic and visually skilled students opportunities to express their strengths while demonstrating their understanding of improv concepts and elements of story structure.

BREAK-THROUGH MOMENTS

Teachers talk about kids. We do and we do it all the time. The observations we make of our students' experiences are important and powerful. They teach us. They inform us whether what we are doing is working or not working. They can be validating, informative, and surprising. They can be impactful when shared with others. The entries below are a few of my experiences from my classroom or from workshops I did with other classes and schools.

Back on Task: (high school)

Once, in the middle of their collaborative writing activities, we had a fire drill. When we were allowed back into the building, I stayed behind my class herding them as best I could through the crowded hallways back into the room. On my way back to the class I still held the disappointment of the interruption to the lesson and now the challenge of getting the students back on task. When I reached the room, I was stunned. To my surprise, notebooks were being rapidly passed around the tables. The class completely reengaged on their own in writing their stories.

A Bit Obsessive: (high school)

There was once a student who was behind grade level in reading and writing, but seemed to be happy and engaged during the collaborative writing activities. Through a conversation with a learning disabilities counselor, I found out that this student was considered so low in reading and writing ability that she was not even tested on standardized tests. That was surprising because she was eagerly composing coherent stories with her group. Well, it was during the individual writing assignments that a surprising issue came to light. It wasn't that she couldn't write, which was previously thought to be the case. She was obsessive about the neatness of her handwriting, which is another issue entirely. After writing one or two sentences she would erase every word on her paper and start again. This did not manifest during the collaborative writing activities as she had to make an offer and pass it, having no time to be self-critical and erase. Having observed this, I stayed with her during the individual story writing encouraging her to "Yes and…" her way to the end of her story, while also blocking her attempts to rip the paper up and start again. In the end, this student now had a few complete writing samples to show her other teachers and counselors, and school personnel had a better understanding of her needs.

Girl Power: (middle school)

This 8th grade class was clearly dominated by the boys. They called out, they demanded attention, and they got it much to the teacher's frustration. The girls were quiet, reserved, did their work quietly, and rarely asked questions. During an 80-minute workshop with this class, all of the girls played "Yes and…Planning." Through this they began to get the hang of "taking attention." Gradually the boys were integrated into the group of girls and the planning continued. The girls did not back down. They continued to offer their ideas confidently and take the attention to speak when they wanted. The teacher was thrilled and the dynamics of the class became more balanced.

Class Clown: (middle school)

The teacher was at wits'-end with a five-foot-tall boy and his minions. He was a class clown who seemed to disrupt class constantly. At the beginning of the workshop he actually tossed his shoe across the floor. During a classroom workshop, the students were introduced to a few of the improv games contained in this book. Two amazing transformations happened. First, the class learned how not to "give their attention" to this kid and his friends. Instead they proceeded to "take the attention" of the teacher back by focusing on the games being introduced. This forced the class clown to continue participating in the hopes of regaining the massive amounts of attention he sought. It was predictable when he started to "deny" in the activities, but he wasn't getting the big laughs he wanted. Instead he was stopping the games as "denying" does and seeing the disappointed glares of the other students. To regain the big laughs and attention, he started to listen to the other students and build off their ideas. He was still "taking attention," but he was now also "giving attention" to others. He learned how to get the attention he wanted, but in a way that allowed the class to continue and everyone to learn.

Speaking Skills: (high school)

Some of the girls I taught were quiet, mostly due to their ethnic and cultural upbringing. They sometimes talked with little more than a whisper. It's probably very frustrating for them, as they were extremely bright, studious, and wanted to contribute in class. Unfortunately, I often found myself asking them to speak louder because I just couldn't hear what they were saying. None of us enjoyed that daily exchange. Well, after about four months of playing Zip-Zap-Zop *(p. 116)* in its various forms, something simple yet wonderful happened. While my back was turned to the class, a girl asked for a pass to the bathroom. I responded, "Sure." Then I heard from the back of the room an astonished but clear voice proclaiming, "You heard me! You've never heard me before! You heard me!" There was one of the quietest girls I taught, beaming and still needing a pass to the bathroom.

Scanning Skills: (high school)

After finishing collaborative written stories for Story-Story, students were asked to circle any words or phrases that indicated the given genre. Within moments one girl excitedly exclaimed that by only reading what she circled, one could tell what the entire story was about. She then proudly took it upon herself to read her circled information to the class to prove her discovery. I was glad she did. I hadn't thought of the impact on scanning skills at that point.

2

BACK IN THE CLASSROOM AGAIN:

Improv as an Instructional Tool

IMPROV IS A FUN, ENERGETIC, DYNAMIC, AND EFFECTIVE WAY TO:

* Develop Literacy Skills: Speaking, Listening, Reading and Writing

* Develop Communication, Performance and Presentation Skills

* Work in Collaboration, Build Effective Teams

* Develop Confidence and Self-Esteem

* Develop Social-Emotional and Interpersonal Skills

* Nurture Creativity, Thinking Out of the Box and Innovation

* Nurture Spontaneity, Thinking on One's Feet, Being Flexible and Adaptable

* Develop Character, Trust, Respect, Tolerance, and Embrace Diversity

* Increase Motivation, Productivity, and Accountability

* Improve Leadership and Negotiation Skills

* Develop Awareness, Focus, Concentration Skills, and Stay Present in the Moment

* Decrease Management Issues and Improve Self-Regulation of Behavior

* Lower Stress and Anxiety in the Learning Environment

* Increase and Deepen Learning

* Structure and Energize Brainstorming Sessions

"IMPROV DOES ALL THAT?"

Yes! These benefits of learning improv might sound exaggerated or unrealistic, but they really are true. The length of the list and use of similar terms illustrates how improv is presented to a wide array of ages and interest groups. From elementary school students to business professionals, improv can develop all of those skills and attributes listed and more. It might be thought that if learning improv can provide all of these benefits, then improv must be a very complex system; or that by providing so many different benefits, improv only superficially addresses the skills. Improv actually does deliver those skills in an effective, efficient and impactful manner. Improv is not complicated and the results are profound.

"AND WITH NO EXTRA EFFORT?"

Neither the students nor the teacher need to focus on individual skills in order for them to develop. The benefits of improv are actually quite easy and straightforward to attain. The teacher needs only to facilitate the games with respect to the rules and structures, and the students need to play them with respect to the rules and structures.

"WHAT IS IMPROV?"

"Theater Games are a process applicable to any field, discipline,
or subject matter which creates a place where full participation,
communication and transformation can take place," (Spolin, 1974).

Many people are most familiar with improv games as zany and hilarious comedic stage performances from theater or TV, but interestingly, improv games were not originally created for actors to be funny. Instead, improv games were created to teach skills and techniques in acting classrooms. It may seem a far stretch to see comedic improv as useful in the classroom, as it looks to be an exercise in complete freedom. However, improv games are actually based on specific rules and structures that nurture an environment of collaboration and allow for spontaneity to exist. It is the structure and rules that make improv an adaptive and useful instructional tool for all teachers. The journey into the academic classroom did not begin with a huge leap off the stage, but simply a broadening of its original purpose: to teach skills and techniques, and more recently, subject area content as well.

Throughout human history improvisation has been an integral component of drama; however, in recent decades improvisation has developed into its own art form called improvisational theater, or improv for short. This development is widely credited to Viola Spolin, who is regarded as the mother of improvisation and internationally recognized as the founder of Theater Games, the basis of improvisational theater. Needing a means to address a specific focus or technical problem while also transcending cultural and ethnic barriers, Spolin began creating theater games while working for the Works Progress Administration's Recreation Project as drama supervisor from 1939 to 1941. She continued creating games through the 1940s and 1950s. These theater games would become standard elements in dramatic instruction and would soon branch off, developing into a new and independent performing art form, improv.

Improvisational theater/improv began its evolution into a distinct art form starting in the 1950s under the direction of Paul Sills, son of Viola Spolin. With specific rules, such as "Yes, and..." and defined structures, two general formats emerged: long-form improv, which may take 40 minutes or more; and short-form improv that consists of short 3- to 5-minute games. Improv should not be confused with improvisational role-playing activities commonly used to explore situations, characters or texts, or to develop scripts, as well as many other purposes. Although improvisational role plays and theater games are unscripted, experiential, and learning-centered, they are not necessarily collaborative or structured by the rule of "Yes, and...". The 3- to 5-minute comedic improv games presented in this book, follow very specific and defined rules and structures. It is adherence to the rules and structures that allow spontaneity to exist and comedy to erupt. It is also adherence to these same rules and structures that will increase student motivation, deepen learning, and develop language arts, social-emotional, and performance skills.

IMPROV IN THE CLASSROOM

From its origins as a classroom strategy to reach culturally diverse learners, improv continues as a pedagogical tool for instruction/training. Improv serves as a collaborative, student-centered, experiential, multi-model approach that motivates, engages, and honors students of diverse backgrounds and educational needs. Improv develops numerous social-emotional, performance, and academic skills. It fosters creativity and community. Improv can be integrated into lessons and support content, and be aligned to standards. What makes improv an amazingly efficient intervention is that all of the benefits are developed simultaneously when the games are played with respect to the rules and structures. By understanding and focusing on the foundational rule of "Yes, and..." many desirable skills will develop. Adherence to the structure of improv games will motivate, engage, and deepen learning. This ability has catapulted improv into the classroom to serve as an effective and efficient intervention. *Chapter 3* explains in great detail how improv can transform the learning environment and nurture the simultaneous development of so many valuable skills, with no extra effort from the teacher.

Teachers of kindergarten-adult have embraced improv as a means to improve instruction, support learning, and improve student outcomes. University medical, law, and business programs have incorporated improvisational training to prepare their students for career-based situations (Berk & Trieber, 2009). University education departments are introducing education students to the benefits of improvisation and the multifaceted role it can play in improving teaching and learning (Cantor, 2003; Sawyer, 2011). Businesses and organizations are seeking ways in which improv can better prepare their leaders and workforce to address individual or organizational performance demands (Sawyer, 2007; Scinto, 2014).

A major impediment holding improv back from taking an even more widespread and consistent role in the classroom is due to a very common misunderstanding of how and why improv works. TV shows such as *Whose Line is it Anyway?* brought great attention to improv, but not an understanding of what it is and how and why it works. Because of this, many people believe improv to be a bunch of fun acting games played by amazingly talented people that produce hilarious results with seemingly no rules. When you watch improv and witness the surprising and funny twists and turns of each game, that view is understandable, but not at all complete. To truly understand improv and reap the educational benefits it can provide, one must understand the process of improv. The process is composed of rules and structures that create the skills, relationships, and the environment necessary for those engaged to consistently produce spontaneous results.

IMPROV AS A PROCESS

*If you can't describe what you are doing as a process, you
don't know what you're doing (W. Edwards Deming).*

The first time I heard that quote, I felt a little defensive. After all, teaching is an art as well as a science. As I had a little more time to reflect upon it, the truth of it became quite clear. As a teacher there were times when I couldn't explain why a certain lesson or intervention worked, but it did and I felt great. Although it may have worked brilliantly, if I couldn't explain what worked and how and why it worked, then I couldn't always repeat the results or expect a co-worker to replicate the results. Unfortunately in education, when that occurs we sometimes decide that such a success is due to the artistry of the specific teacher, when it *can* actually be explained, replicated and shared when one examines the instructional design, facilitation skills, and other instructional methods used. By using the artistry of teaching as a crutch to avoid understanding the process, we lose the opportunity to sustain and replicate those amazing and valuable results achieved in the classroom.

Improv, being a performing art, is often treated the same way. I am not saying improv is also a science, but improv is based upon a very distinct process. Improv follows specific rules and defined structures. Attitudes that profess that improv cannot be defined because it is always different merely focus on a resulting performance and not on the process, which is consistent. When this process is understood, when the rules and structures are respected and practiced, then the resulting skill development can be sustained and replicated, although the individual performances will always be different. This is important for three reasons.

▶ When improv is defined by its unique final products or performances, it becomes undefinable and therefore not replicable. Understanding improv as a process allows it to be recognized as an instructional tool capable of repeatedly producing desired outcomes.

▶ An understanding of how improv so masterfully develops skills will dispel fears that it is only for the talented and funny. The process of improv reveals the simplicity and source of its power. Understanding that the results are produced by simply following the rules and structures can reduce a sense of intimidation one might feel when introducing an art form to students who have no prior training.

▶ When the focus is only on the outcome of producing a hilarious and energy-filled performance, the process of improv is often compromised. Understanding improv as a process will help ensure that it is implemented correctly so it may serve as an effective educational intervention, developing writing fluency as well as many other essential literacy, social-emotional, and performance skills.

MISUNDERSTANDINGS

If the games are facilitated without a clear understanding of how improv so effectively and efficiently produces the many desired skills and attributes they seek, the teacher is prone to purposefully or inadvertently change aspects of the structure or bypass the rules. These seemingly innocuous decisions may be catastrophic, debilitating the power of improv and thus impeding or nullifying its ability to produce the desired skills and attributes. The essential role that improv's rules and structures play cannot be misunderstood or minimized.

1. Improv works because people "just get up and do it"

This common misperception believes that improv helps people develop skills by merely providing the opportunity to "work together, take risks, be creative, etc...". "They're getting up there and doing it." There are many other activities and programs available that merely provide opportunities to team build or be creative. The power of improv to transform the individual and the culture of a class is far more effectual than a mere opportunity to participate in a creative or team-building exercise. Improv develops the underlying skills and attributes for the individual and the group to actually become collaborative, creative, adaptable, etc. Not only does improv fail to differentiate itself from other activities when its process is minimized, but if improv is taught and later replicated without adherence to the rules and structures such as "Yes, and...," the sought-after skills will not be achieved immediately or at all.

2. Improv works because it's fun

Another misconception regarding improv that leads to the rules and structures being minimized or completely ignored is that improv works because it is fun. Fun is only one aspect of why students may be motivated to participate. For all those moments when a particular game is not feeling fun for a student or the audience, there are a number of other equally motivating qualities of improv that sustain motivation and engagement. Fun is only one of the five essential human needs (Glasser, 1998) met by improv that increases motivation, engagement, and helps to deepen learning. In addition to that, "having fun," although a motivating factor, is not directly responsible for skill development.

This notion that improv works because it is fun becomes detrimental when teachers will sometimes ignore the rules and structures in order to keep the momentum, or "fun," of the game going. In some cases, they make the harmful decision to increase the "fun" by eliminating students who are learning the games thinking it will even increase the "fun" by calling people "out." Although this may be an aspect of a game at a higher level of performance, when students are still learning improv, this practice simply denies that student and the group the opportunity to develop the intended skills.

Improv is not some magically fun activity in which all students immediately have fun at the moment they start playing a game. In improv, it is the adherence and practice of following the rules and structures that produce the humorous situations as well as develop the skills that ultimately allow the individual and the group to experience "fun."

3. Choose the Funniest Game

It is not uncommon for a teacher, eager to introduce improv into their classroom, to choose a game because they or their students are familiar with it from seeing it performed on stage or TV. Problems quickly arise because many improv games create situations or scenes that immediately require adequate knowledge of drama techniques such as staging, blocking, endowment, movement and character development. Also required is an understanding of basic story elements and structure, as well as the rules of improv and structure of the specific game. The game's level of difficulty becomes apparent and the teacher quickly starts side coaching to "Just keep going." Now the rules of improv are being ignored, negating any of the powerful benefits hoped to be gained. If curricular content was integrated into the game, its accuracy is also minimized with a side coaching like, "Don't worry if the scene/story makes sense." So, with no chance of experiencing the power improv can have on the growth of an individual and a class or in how content can be successfully integrated, teachers quickly lose interest and abandon improv as a useful educational pedagogy. Unfortunately, this chain of events can also occur when experienced theater/improv teachers/actors give workshops at schools to teachers and students. They sometimes become driven by a perceived need to facilitate a sense of energy and enjoyment, instead of teaching improv.

These misperceptions can result in improv being confused with or indistinguishable from any other game, activity, or icebreaker. Improv becomes just a fun break from the norm with no transformative results. The *Improv 'n Ink* sequence presented in this book will help the teacher avoid this situation and experience the efficiency and effectiveness of improv. When understood, improv can serve as an impactful instructional tool in the classroom. The following chapters provide detailed explanations, insights and research of how and why improv is capable of increasing writing fluency, while also developing additional literacy and social-emotional skills, and increasing engagement, motivation, and learning.

> ▶ *Chapter 3* describes how and why improv's rules and structures develop skills, increase motivation, reach learners, and deepen learning.

> ▶ *Chapter 4* explains how the *Improv 'n Ink* game sequence enables students to increase their writing fluency.

3

THE POWER WITHIN IMPROV

Understanding Rules and Structures

Improv is powerful. It is transformative to both the individual and the group. It can engage and motivate learners, and nurture impressive skill development effectively and efficiently. It is not, however, complex to facilitate or perform. In order to reap the immense educational benefits improv can deliver, the teacher and the students only need to understand and follow *one rule* and a *four-part structure*.

THE RULE OF "YES, AND..."

Both the comedic performances and the invaluable skills that result from improv are because of the rule of *"Yes, and..."*. *"Yes, and..."* is more than just an improv rule. It is the foundation of improv. In the *Improv 'n Ink* sequence of games it is first practiced as an external prompt as demonstrated in the game Yes, And-Planning:

Audience Suggestion:	Plan a trip.
Student 1:	Hey let's plan a trip.
Student 2:	Yes, and we can charter our own plane.
Student 3:	Yes, and we all skydive down to our hotel location.

"Yes, and..." is the most essential and powerful rule of improv. It is first introduced and practiced as an external prompt, but quickly becomes internalized, unspoken but present in every offer given. "Yes, and…" allows a collaborative environment to emerge. By saying or thinking, "Yes, and…" individuals must listen to and accept the preceding idea and then add to it. Their idea is then accepted by another who adds their idea to it. This is practiced repeatedly.

OTHER RULES ARE REMINDERS TO "YES, AND..."

My intention is not to be groundbreaking or controversial by presenting "Yes, and..." as the only rule to improv, but treating it as such may be helpful when teaching improv to those with little or no experience. "Yes, and..." is recognized as the foundational rule of improv; however, it is often only briefly explained as accepting another's idea, then presented on equal footing with numerous other rules. Minimizing the role and impact of "Yes, and..." and thinking that other rules need to be learned, understood, and followed separately makes improv seem unnecessarily complicated and difficult to learn. It might be beneficial to view these other rules of improv not as separate rules equal to "Yes, and...", but as succinct side coachings given to achieve "Yes, and..." without interrupting the momentum of the game. Some of these commonly cited improv rules are as follows:

Don't Deny

A denial occurs when a student does not "Yes, and...". They fail to build upon the preceding offer and consequently deny another's "offer." When a denial occurs, it's as if the brakes were slammed on the creative process. Momentum stops. The scene or game is halted. Examples of denials are found in the game, Yes, and-Planning, located in *Chapter 6 (pp.75-76)*.

Don't Fight

This is also a form of denial. Physical or verbal fighting stops the scene. It is the denial of the preceding offer. "Let's run." "No." "Yes." "No." The scene is over. Creativity has stopped. "Yes, and..." has stopped.

Don't Ask Questions

Asking questions that offer no new information is another form of denial. Questions can come in many forms, but the results are usually the same. "Yes, and..." was ignored. New information was not offered. The scene was slowed or stopped.

Keep the Scene Moving Forward

The purpose of this rule is to ensure that the action of a scene is not stopped through a form of denial. Keeping a scene moving is actually accomplished by using "Yes, and..."

Don't Mug

Mugging is an attempt to get a laugh from the audience by making a funny expressive face. Again, this is not "Yes, and...". It is not listening or building off an idea. It is instead making a facial expression that judges or comments on the preceding offer. It is stopping the momentum and taking a selfish moment to achieve a laugh at the expense of others, the process, and the game.

Don't Go for the Joke

Again, by going for the joke, "Yes, and..." is ignored. The joke may or may not get a laugh, but what is certain is that going for the joke stopped the process. Others were not validated, skills were not achieved, and objectives were not met, because an individual wanted to be "funny." Improv is collaborative. It is not stand-up comedy.

Don't Judge Yourself or Others

Again, this is really more of a side coaching than a separate rule. "Yes, and…" suspends judgment by requiring the acceptance of the previous offer whether it is from another or from yourself. Just build upon the preceding idea and see where it goes.

Give Yourself Permission/Go Big

Give yourself permission to offer big, daring, inventive, out-of-the-box, exciting ideas. Give yourself permission to "Yes, and…"

Make the Other Person Look Good

Again, this is often presented as a separate rule, but it is obviously an outcome of "Yes, and…". If you want to make your partner look good, then accept their idea and build off it. It is denial in its many forms that will invalidate the other person in front of others.

Give and Take

Give and Take or Giving and Taking Attention is a common intro acting game, side coaching, and improv rule. This rule supports "Yes, and…" by helping individuals effectively communicate their offers. It nurtures awareness that one must give their attention so others can "Yes, and…;" and that they must effectively and respectfully take attention so they themselves can "Yes, and…" A student gives attention by stopping to speak and directing their physical energy and eye contact to the designated individual. In order to "take the attention" from another, the individual needs to speak with conviction and loudly enough to be heard, so that other students stop speaking and turn their focus to the individual attempting to "take the attention" from them.

STAY FOCUSED ON "YES, AND…"

Using the above rules/side coachings to stay focused on "Yes, and…" increases student engagement and allows for valuable performance skills to develop. For example, the teacher does not direct the students to practice trusting each other or being confident. The teacher will simply remind the students to "Yes, and…". Individuals will be more receptive to "Remember to, 'Yes, and…'" instead of "We need to work on trusting each other" or "Come on, get some confidence." Side coachings like, "Denial," or "Don't ask questions," are concise reminders that will not severely interrupt the momentum of the game. These phrases help the teacher to avoid rambling on with, "What are you doing? Why are you asking questions? Don't ask questions. That's a denial. Alright, come on. Keep going." Students will be more receptive to these succinct side coachings than what may be perceived as a teacher nagging or "picking on them." Hearing "Give and take" or "Take the attention" will not be received as defensively as "Give other people a chance to speak," or "Speak louder, we can't hear you."

"YES, AND..." DEVELOPS SKILLS

Yes, and..." will produce academic, social-emotional, and performance skills like those listed at the beginning of this chapter. Because "Yes and..." is responsible for the development of all of these skills, the explanations may begin to sound repetative or redundant. Please feel free to use this section like a manual, skipping to skills of particular interest.

* ## Collaboration/Teamwork/Cooperation

The terms teamwork or cooperation are sometimes used interchangeably with the term collaboration; however, collaboration is actually quite different and is responsible for the development of the many valuable skills improv offers. Collaboration is sometimes simply defined as students working together, but this can lead to the misconception that collaborative learning is the same as cooperative learning or teamwork, and consequently be dismissed as a method already practiced in most classrooms. The key difference between collaboration, teamwork, and cooperation is that cooperative groups, as well as teams, are directed by a leader, with group members usually having specific roles and defined tasks that often develop specific outcomes. Within a collaborative group, authority is shared; there is an acceptance of responsibility among the group members for the group's actions. The contributions and abilities of the group's members are highlighted (Panitz, 1996). With group members functioning as equals, the teacher acts not from an authoritarian position but as a guide or coach, empowering the group members, who are given more flexible and complex tasks.

The collaborative nature of improv structures is due to the rule of "Yes, and...". Through its consistent practice in every improv game, "Yes, and..." teaches individuals to listen to a preceding idea and build upon it, not to deny it or make fun of it. Individuals working collaboratively begin to feel safe as a sense of trust develops. They begin to trust their ability to contribute, their peers' abilities to contribute, and the fact that no ideas will be rejected. With a sense of threat or anxiety fading, students experience a growth in their self-esteem, as well as confidence, trust, and respect toward themselves and others. "Yes, and..." nurtures the individual and group skills necessary for a collaborative relationship to exist and function. Once established, collaboration with its ongoing exchanges and interactions between group members drives creativity, innovation, and many other skills, first within the improv structures and later in the individual's or group's performance in class, work and life.

* ## Communication: Speaking and Listening Skills

Listening Skills: "Yes, and..." supports the development of deep listening, which enhances the outcomes of instruction. Deep listening, a skill and concept originating in improvisational theater, is practiced and developed through participation in improv exercises. The skill addresses the habit people of not listening completely to what someone is saying because they are already thinking of what they will say next. In improvisation, new ideas are born when one presents an offer that is an elaboration on preceding offers. In order to present the best new offer, one must have fully listened to what was spoken. Listening skills are further strengthened by the practice of *Giving and Taking Attention*, which reminds students to turn their body, including eye contact, and direct their physical energy when listening to an individual making an offer. This enables one to better hear and also understand the offer, while demonstrating a posture that conveys respect.

Speaking Skills: "Yes and..." necessitates that offers are communicated effectively between students. *Give and Take* fosters an awareness that one must not only give their attention so others can make an offer, but that they must effectively and respectfully take attention so they themselves can make their contribution. When an individual takes the attention to make an offer, that offer will need to be loud enough to be heard, articulate enough to be understood, and possess the appropriate tone to convey its intended meaning. The next offer will be built upon that offer and will be responsive to its words and emotional tone. Improv helps develop the individual's speaking skills by enabling them to gain an acute awareness not only of what they say and if it is loud enough, but also how it is said and how that tone or intonation will influence the responding offer.

* Creativity/Innovation/ Thinking Out of the Box/Risk Taking

Improv demonstrates that new and innovative ideas are not created within a vacuum but are most often built upon existing knowledge. Creative or new solutions usually originate from one or many incremental changes made to an existing idea. Within improv, the rule of "Yes, and..." allows creativity and innovation to flourish both collaboratively and later individually. "Yes, and..." gives a structure to collaboration in which incremental changes are made on each offer. Through the consistent practice of "Yes, and..." individuals learn to accept an idea from another. They suspend their judgment and relinquish a sense of control. They remain present in the moment at all times. Finally, adapting to a new set of objectives or circumstances, they give an offer based upon the preceding offer. Their new offer will take an idea or scene into a new, unscripted, spontaneous direction. This ability to accept an offer, the flexibility to incrementally add to that offer sending it out to other members of the group to do the same, results in new, creative, "out of the box" ideas. "Yes, and..." structures the exchanges and interactions of collaboration that produce creativity and innovation.

* Flexible Thinking/Reacting and Adapting Quickly/Negotiating

The rule of "Yes, and..." and improv's structure offer the opportunity to develop the skills that enables one to be flexible in one's thinking: to react, adapt, and negotiate. "Yes, and..." builds the confidence and trust in one's self to put an idea forward. Fluency of thought keeps the ideas/offers flowing. The suspension of judgment and the ability to relinquish control in a situation keeps those ideas/offers changing and appropriately adapting. Individuals build from offer to offer: listening, offering, and listening again. They become comfortable adapting to changing circumstances quickly and with direction. Working collaboratively within improv structures enables one to learn and practice the improv rule that produces these desired skills.

* Fluency: Thought, Speech and Writing

"Yes, and…" serves as a prompt to students to continually add their thoughts, thus increasing fluency of thought, speech, and writing. "Yes, and…" is introduced and practiced in the game Yes, And-Planning as an external prompt as students are directed to say "Yes, and…" before each offer. "Yes, and…" is then practiced and reinforced in all other improv games as an internal prompt with students thinking "Yes, and…" before giving their offer. Serving to structure and drive a student's internal dialogue when thinking, speaking, and writing, "Yes, and…" helps students connect, grow, and express their own thoughts and ideas.

* Focus/Awareness/Staying in the Moment

Improv offers the repetitive, well-paced, and consistent practice of the rule "Yes, and…," which applies to all types of offers, whether they be verbal, physical, or emotional. "Yes, and…" requires the students to stay in the moment so they can be fully aware of and understand the preceding offer from another player. If a student is instead focused elsewhere, like what they are doing after class or planning how to take the scene in the direction they want, they will in some form deny the preceding offer. The denial will result in the immediate feedback of an impeded or stopped scene/game. The student will quickly become aware of the need for them to remain in the moment at all times so they can "Yes, and…"

* Problem Solving/Conflict Resolution

Problems and conflicts arise for many reasons, but they often remain unsolved due to a failure in communication and an inability to work together to achieve a solution. The practice of "Yes, and…," "Giving and Taking Attention," and certain improv game structures can improve the skills needed to achieve resolution. With "Yes, and…" there is no denial, dismissing, or negating of another's offer. There is no fighting. By fostering attitudes of trust, respect, and confidence individuals can come together as a group and engage to find solutions. "Yes, and…" requires an individual to listen fully, stay in the moment, be flexible and adaptive, and receive and build upon the preceding offer. The individual who ignored, dismissed, or invalidated another's offer through denial is no longer in a position of respect in which they may have been in a noncollaborative setting. They are now solely responsible for bringing the collaborative process to a stop and impeding the process of finding a solution or reaching a resolution.

Everyone involved shares in the responsibility to give attention and take attention so problems can be addressed and solutions created. Giving attention supports "Yes, and…" by reminding individuals and groups that they must not go on and on lecturing, focused only on their views, visions, or needs. They instead must give their attention completely to others so they may also express themselves. Taking attention reminds the individual and group that they must not sit silent in frustration. It is their responsibility to actively and definitively take the attention to express their views.

Improv game structures encourage and guide individuals to work toward a solution. One-word story structures compel individuals to listen to each and every word the other says in order to work together toward a solution to their story. More complex story games and scene-based games reinforce flexibility, adaptability, and responsiveness as the group works collaboratively to resolve their storyline. The three-step story structure, whereby the essential elements of a story are clearly established (CROW: character, relationship, objective, where), a problem arises, and a solution or resolution is found, is analogous with the identification of key elements of an issue, acknowledgment of the conflict, and the need to work toward a solution.

* Self Esteem/Trust/Confidence

Both *"Yes, and…"* and *Giving and Taking Attention* helps develop a sense of trust, confidence, and self-esteem. By participating in collaborative improv games individuals are consistently practicing to accept ideas and offers made by another. They learn to trust that they will be able to build upon that idea and that their new idea will be accepted by the next student. Through this practice, individuals begin to trust peers they may never have worked with before, spoken to before, or even have shown any respect for prior to working in collaboration. With each received offer, individuals repeatedly ignore or work through any desire to be defensive, critical, and judgmental, or simply negating of an offer. This practice of accepting the offers of others eventually translates to one's acceptance and trust in their own offers. They will discover a level of personal trust, acceptance, and confidence in their own ideas that they may have not felt before. As they engage in their own thinking, speaking, writing, or performing, individuals embrace a sense of assurance that when they continue to add their own ideas one after another, those ideas will be acceptable to themselves and others.

In order to effectively practice "Yes, and…," students are simultaneously practicing giving and taking attention, which requires them to stay aware and present in the moment. This soon translates into the confidence that they are in the moment, paying attention, knowing what is going on, and are thus able to make valuable and relevant contributions.

* Spontaneity/ Thinking on Your Feet /Extemporaneous

Both the rule of "Yes, and…" and improv structures support the development of these skills. Game structures, requiring two or more people, create the opportunity to consistently practice "Yes, and…," thereby developing fluency of thought and the suspension of judgment necessary to offer spontaneous and extemporaneous ideas. Games that include multiple people will further increase the pressure and pace of giving and taking attention so offers can be made, thus strengthening these skills.

* Self-Awareness/Discipline/Regulation of Behavior

The application of *"Yes and…"* and *Giving and Taking Attention* can help teachers manage and avoid classroom management issues. The application of these rules empowers students to regulate their own behavior and to realize the control they have over their learning environment and experience. If one or more individuals are disrupting the group, a teacher usually tries to regain their position of authority by retaking the attention of the students.

When the teacher fails, students who do want to engage in the lesson are also left frustrated by the teacher's failure. Instead of this often exhausting and sometimes futile approach, the teacher may remind the group that they have the power to give attention to those disruptive individuals and the power to take their attention away from them. This awareness of the power to "give," as well as "take attention" can be quite empowering to those students who do want to participate. The students are reminded of their control or power in the learning environment. They can very simply not give their attention to the disruptive student(s) and instead give it to the teacher. Essentially, the students take the teacher's attention away from the disruptive individual and give that attention to themselves by remaining focused on the lesson or teacher. The power of this technique is the perception of empowerment it gives to the student. When individuals/groups understand the power they actually have, positive results can be immediate.

When attention is "taken away" from the class clown or attention-seeking individual, they are forced to reassess how to get attention. The rules have changed and so may their behavior. Now disruptive attention seekers may learn to receive the attention they need through participating in class, not by disrupting it. As the once-disruptive individual begins to participate in improv games, they will initially try to disrupt them by denying. It will happen, and they may still get laughs even if the other students are trying not to give them the attention; however, eventually those denying individuals realize that the biggest laughs, the most fun, and sought-after attention are enjoyed best by those who play by the rules. The once disruptive student continues to seek the intrinsic reward of attention or empowerment; however, they do this by following the rules of improv. This helps them become a productive member of the class and develop the beneficial skills nurtured by improv that can improve their performance in other areas as well.

IMPROV STRUCTURES

In addition to its rules, improv structures make improv the unique, effective, and powerful instructional activity that it is, distinguishing it from games, icebreakers, and other instructional activities. In improv, the term structure may refer to a specific game, type of game, or the framework all improv games share in common. For example, structure may pertain to the framework for the specific game of Freeze Tag and any of its numerous variations. Structure may also apply to the general framework that improv games follow:

1. The director chooses a game.
2. The audience is asked to offer one or more of the following elements of CROW (character, relationship, objective or where) for the game.
3. The players then use the audience's suggestions as they perform a selected game.
4. After the game, the players evaluate what worked and what did not work within the performance, either as a group and/or individually.

Although not generally thought of as part of the improv structure, group and self-assessment is an integral component of improv and should not be taken for granted. This assessment stage occurs after each game and is performed whether an individual is learning improv or is professionally performing improv. Instruction, whether it be in the classroom or in the sports arena, does not always prepare an individual or group to self-assess. Think of the teacher that just returns a test paper with a numerical grade or the coach who just calls the team together and tells them what they need to work on. The time to assess provides the opportunity to learn productive language when offering feedback to others as well to one's self. It guides and supports the learning process. It is a motivational aspect of improv and becomes a transformational skill that one integrates into life. An individual trained in improv will find themself regularly asking, "OK, what worked and what didn't work?"

STRUCTURES MOTIVATE

Our first thoughts when we hear that improv motivates individuals might go something like this: "The students are playing games, having fun, and laughing. Of course they're motivated." Educators realize that motivation is crucial to the successful mastery of standards, and also that games that produce enjoyment and laughter are powerful and effective motivators. Improv, however, provides more than just fun by addressing five basic human needs. William Glasser, author of *Choice Theory* (1998), categorized these needs as survival, belonging/connectedness, power/competence, autonomy, and fun. Although we are most familiar with the motivational power of having fun, the other needs Glasser identifies are equally addressed by participation in improv games. Specifically, improv games address Glasser's concepts in the following ways:

1. SURVIVAL

Survival needs are met when the classroom environment is kept free from both physical and emotional threats. Current neuroscience reveals that when threat is perceived, students will have great difficulty learning (Jensen, 1998; Sousa, 2011). Improv helps reduce or eliminate a sense of threat and anxiety by creating a collaborative learning environment. Social interactions practiced during games are framed by the rule of "Yes, and...". Each time a student's offer is accepted and built upon, they gain a sense of trust and confidence in themself and others. They are validated and their individual uniqueness valued. With the sense of threat dispelled, they enter an appropriate physical and emotional state conducive to learning.

2. FUN/ENJOYMENT

Having fun deepens and strengthens learning while helping students maintain a desire to learn (Sullo, 2007). Improv can be fun and enjoyable for those acting as the audience or actively performing the game. Unexpected offers, twists, and choices can be hilarious for all involved. There are, however, also plenty of times when improv may not feel fun for the audience or the student. A boring scene, a painful performance, that excruciating moment when a player freezes is just not fun for anyone. Nevertheless, improv still motivates people to keep going, try again, and look forward to the next session. Improv is an exceptionally powerful motivator because it meets four other essential needs. When fun fails, people still gain a sense of survival, belonging, empowerment, and competence, keeping them motivated and engaged.

3. AUTONOMY

An individual's desire and need for autonomy in the learning process is present from the earliest grades and increases as they age. This need for autonomy has been identified as an integral force behind student motivation (Anderman and Leake, 2005). Improv offers individuals the opportunity to develop and sense their autonomy through self-expression, choice, and creativity. Fostering a supportive relationship and acting as a coach or guide, the teacher creates a learning environment that gives the students the freedom to construct their own knowledge, while providing the elements of structure that effectively scaffold a co-constructive process (Sawyer, 2004, March & June). Through improv, individuals make offers, create spontaneously, and engage in self and peer assessment. Improv supports the students' need for autonomy in the learning process.

4. BELONGING

As discussed in the previous chapter, the collaborative nature of improv creates a sense of community. "Building a spirit of connection and community is essential to creating a need-satisfying school characterized by high achievement (Sullo, 2007. p. 8)." Individuals who feel threatened or marginalized will at best struggle to learn, if they try at all (Jensen, 2005). Students who feel marginalized in a learning environment may develop a lack of trust not only in their peers' but in their own abilities, thus impacting their self-esteem. Through collaboration, however, a learning community is created and nurtured. Individuals gain and develop a trust and confidence in their own and their peers' abilities through collaborative work, thus building a community and sense of belonging.

5. POWER/COMPETENCE

The need for power or competency can be satisfied through assessments that empower the individual. In a 1999 interview, Richard J. Stiggins, a leader in educational assessment design, stated, "When students are involved in the assessment process, though, they can come to see themselves as competent learners (Sparks, 1999, p.55)." Stiggins (2011) supports the use of formative assessments as a means to inform the teacher of a student's progress and involve the students in the assessment process. This empowerment of the student through the assessment process has shown increases in student achievement, especially among struggling students, (Black & William, 1998 as cited in Stiggins, 2007). To create an environment where individuals become engaged in the assessment process, the following strategies are suggested by Stiggins (2007). These strategies are central to improv and are further supported by the specific design of the sequence of games in this book.

Define Clear Learning Goals

Important for an individual's sense of control over the learning and assessment process is an understanding of what the intended learning goals for each activity are. The activities in this book are scaffolded to allow both the teacher and the student to focus on specific skills. Each activity builds upon or reinforces the skills presented in the previous one. These clear learning goals are presented to the student in the following ways:

1. At the beginning of the game, the teacher introduces how the game and the involved skills are relevant to the student.

2. During the modeling of the games, the teacher asks students to demonstrate the game to the group. These students are learning the games as they go, so they model both their mistakes and successes.

3. Learning goals are reinforced through the coaching or guidance a teacher gives while the students are engaged in an improv game.

4. Learning goals are again defined through the descriptive feedback, modeled by the teacher and given by the students themselves, as well as their peers. This feedback specifically targets the intended skills.

5. Through the use of activity-specific rubrics that can be used as a guide for self, peer, or teacher assessment, students gain an awareness of their growth and proficiency level of specific skills.

Encourage Responsibility/Accountability

A student's acceptance of responsibility and accountability in the learning process is crucial to their motivation, as well as to the desired outcomes. Through improv, individuals collaborate, functioning as equals within a group, realizing that they are accountable to their peers and themselves for their effort and performance. There is no avoiding their responsibility as there is no opportunity to wait for a more accomplished individual to just do it for them, which frequently occurs in cooperative groups or teams.

Individual and group accountability and productivity are further strengthened by the sense of empowerment gained through participation in improv structures or games. Through personal self-evaluation, and group feedback sessions, students are involved in their own assessment, thus empowering their progress and performance. This sense of empowerment increases their motivation to participate, which in turn strengthens their sense of responsibility and accountability to themselves and to the group. Productivity is positively affected.

Supportive Relationships

With improv, a supportive relationship develops as teachers guide individuals through the activities. This in turn may also increase a student's motivation. As described in the Autonomy section, teachers serve as coaches or guides when facilitating improv, allowing students to explore and create. In addition, a sense of empowerment and competence is gained as teachers provide clear learning goals and precise guidance. Teachers offer positive and descriptive feedback to the students at the conclusion of each activity so that students can improve their performance the next time. The teacher models how to articulate this positive and descriptive style of feedback for the students so they can offer it to their peers and to themselves, thus strengthening a sense of connectedness. This positive and supportive teacher/student relationship fostered by improv satisfies Glasser's (1998) basic human needs, thus increasing motivation and strengthening the learning environment.

RULES AND STRUCTURES TOGETHER

ENGAGE DIVERSE POPULATIONS

Teachers are routinely asked how they are addressing the educational needs of various student populations. Targeting each population separately can be overwhelming. Just as improv can simultaneously develop many valuables skills, it can also simultaneously meet the needs of various populations of learners.

Diversity

With its origins in the theater games created by Viola Spolin to overcome cultural differences among immigrant groups, improv also addresses issues of diversity and cultural relevance. The games presented in this book offer individuals of diverse ethnic, racial, and socio-economic backgrounds the opportunity to create stories/scenes based upon their interests and life experiences, as well as their educational and curricular exposure. This inclusive nature of improv is supported by the rule of "Yes, and…". The rule of "Yes, and…" helps build trust and respect among individuals. Each offer, regardless of the other student's background, is respectfully listened to, accepted, and built upon, providing a sense of validation and respect. Their diverse backgrounds are revealed and honored through their offers during the games.

Special Needs/At Risk

Individuals with special needs or those who are considered at risk or marginalized benefit from improv. The practice of "Yes, and…" can help close gaps in literacy skills that may be impeding their writing. They benefit from the spirit of collaboration, as it dispels anxiety or stress they may have perceived in instructional situations or learning environments. Students can gain an essential trust and confidence in their own abilities that may be lacking, thus enabling them to reengage and more fully participate in the learning process.

Girls

We strive to empower our female students and encourage their participation and achievement. The collaborative nature of improv can help girls/women find their voice and the strength and confidence to participate as equals side by side with their male peers.

Boys

More recently we have set our focus on reengaging our male students who benefit from active learning, movement, teamwork, risk taking, and surprise; as well as scaffoldings and structures that allow them to evaluate themselves so they can navigate through their learning experience (Reichert & Hawley, 2010). Improv games meet those criteria.

New Generations

We are sensitizing ourselves to the needs of the current generations of students who have grown up with technology. These students enjoy learning actively, experientially, and in social and collaborative environments that invite emotional openness. Their limited attention span is engaged by improv's spontaneous and rapidly paced nature that offers students immediate response and feedback (Berk & Trieber, 2009). Improv provides such a learning experience.

DEEPENS LEARNING

The concepts, structures and collaborative nature of improv also provide teachers with strategies that promote deep learning (Campbell, 1998; Entwistle, 2004 as cited in Berk and Trieber 2009). Four criteria for deep learning as defined by Rhem (1995) are met through participation in improv:

1. **Motivational Context**: Improv addresses five basic human needs that drive motivation. These are survival, belonging/connectedness, autonomy, competence/power, and fun/enjoyment.

2. **Learner Activity:** Improv games are active and participatory by nature. They are learner centered, experiential, and embrace inductive discovery.

3. **Interaction with Others:** Improv is collaborative. It not only requires collaboration but it also offers the structure and skill development for collaboration to occur.

4. **Well-Structured Knowledge:** Improv provides a learning environment of inductive discovery. Drawing upon their existing knowledge base and own experience, students construct knowledge through improv as they explore, synthesize, apply, and demonstrate their comprehension of content, creating new and sometime hilarious results. Through active participation in improv, students and teachers create an instructional experience that leads to constructivist learning for deep understanding of the content presented (Sawyer, 2006).

DIFFERENTIATES INSTRUCTION

In an attempt to meet the learning needs of individual students, improv offers a means to differentiate instruction in a number of ways. First, when aligned with Gardner's Multiple Intelligences (1993), the improv games in this sequence alone address most of the intelligences seen in the following chart. Improv also reaches individual students through its ability to meet five basic human needs essential for motivation (Glasser, 1998). Improv can also fit easily into evidence-based instructional designs that support differentiation as presented in *Chapter 5*.

Table 3.1 Alignment of Games to Gardner's Multiple Intelligences

CORE GAMES	Verbal Linguistic	Logical Mathematical	Visual Spatial	Musical-Rhythmic	Bodily Kinesthetic	Inter-personal	Intra-personal
Yes…And	X					X	
We Are	X			X	**X	X	
Volley Word	X			X		X	
Did You Hear…!	X	*X			**X	X	***X
Story-Story!	X	*X			**X	X	***X

ADDITIONAL GAMES	Verbal Linguistic	Logical Math	Visual Spatial	Musical-Rhythmic	Bodily Kines-thetic	Inter-personal	Intra-personal
Zip-Zap-Zop!	X			X	X	X	
Yes, and...flow			X	X	X	X	
Freeze Frame	X		X		X	X	
Freeze Tag	X		X		X	X	

* Story-Story and Did You Hear the One About... can be adapted for students to write collaborative or individual math story problems.

** Teachers may allow students to add movement while they tell their portion of the story. Movement is added by the student while they remain in place. This type of movement does not involve the student moving around the room.

*** Intrapersonal skills are honored with the use of the individual improv writing activities.

WHEN RULES AND STRUCTURES ARE COMPROMISED

When structures are compromised, the potential benefits that improv so profoundly and efficiently produce are diminished or negated. The following notes and chart show how some seemingly innocuous decisions can have catastrophic results.

A FEW NOTES ABOUT STEP 4:

1. Concerned that students might feel uncomfortable during feedback, teachers sometimes skip this opportunity. If improv is being facilitated correctly, its collaborative nature will create a safe and supportive learning environment. With the teacher's guidance and modeling of effective language orientation for critiquing performance, as described in *Chapter 5*, a feedback session should not be uncomfortable.

2. Some teachers may feel the need to keep control and offer all feedback themselves. If this is done because of a lack of time, then it is important that the period of feedback be firmly understood as part of the structure and not something to skip to keep the "fun" going. Without this debriefing time, much of improv's benefits are lost. If the teacher is not allowing the class to offer feedback because they are hesitant to give up a sense of control, the collaborative sense that improv brings to a group and the guidance offered in *Chapter 5* will help the teacher shift from an authoritarian role to a coaching role without compromising their professional boundaries.

3. The rubrics offered in this book serve the instructor and the students as a visual tool as they learn and practice each game. They are not designed to create summative numerical grades for performances. The purpose of these rubrics is to enable the students to gain an awareness of the specific skills developed in each game, monitor progress, and learn appropriate and productive ways to give specific feedback to themselves and others.

Table 3.2 Compromised Structures

Phases Within Game	Common Missteps by Facilitator & Results	Benefits Lost
1) Choose Game	Instructor chooses a game too complex. - Students become overwhelmed - Frustration and management issues arise - Improv rules not practiced	*Skill Development* *Motivation:* fun, belonging, autonomy, competence *Engage:* diverse populations differentiation *Deep Learning*
2) Audience Gives Offer	Instructor provides offer. - Students in audience not engaged	*Motivation:* fun, belonging *Engage:* diverse populations *Responsibility/Accountability*
3) Students Follow Specific Game Structure	Instructor directs students to push through game without respect to essential rules and structures. - Rules and structures not practiced	*Skill Development* *Motivation:* fun, belonging, autonomy *Responsibility/Accountability* *Engage:* diverse populations differentiation *Deep Learning*
4) Post-Game Feedback/ Assessment	Instructor gives all feedback. Does not allow for peer or self-evaluation. - Development of self-assessment is impeded - Does not allow for feedback session - Supportive relationship with teachers does not develop - Improv proficiency is delayed or unachieved	*Motivation:* autonomy, competence *Responsibility/Accountability* *Engage:* diverse populations *Deep Learning*

4

IMPROV 'N INK IN ACTION:

How Improv Develops Writing Fluency

When I learned that students had transferred the concept of "Yes, and..." to classroom writing assignments, I realized that in addition to exciting stories of student success, positive outcomes from surveys, and encouraging statements from students, it could now be possible to collect quantitative evidence to show whether or not improv was increasing the length of students' writing. When the opportunity arose, two research studies were conducted focusing on whether or not writing fluency was impacted from this scaffolded sequence of improv games and improv-writing activities. Study 1 involved an experimental group and a comparison group at an inner-city high school. It occurred during a 6-week summer program for a total of 570 minutes of instruction and practice. Study 2 compared the growth demonstrated by two classes for four months prior to being exposed to the game sequence and then immediately thereafter. Taking place in a suburban high school during the regular school year, students practiced the sequence over the course of eight class periods for a total of 180 minutes of instruction and practice. The data collected from both studies (DeMichele, 2015) produced the following findings:

1. Students demonstrated significant growth in the length of their writing over the comparison group in Study 1 and the comparison time period in Study 2. The special-needs students in Study 1 and the special-need/at-risk population in Study 2 showed even greater growth over the regular-education populations.

    a. The regular-education students in Study 1 demonstrated a 52% increase in word usage and a 32% increase in sentence usage over the comparison group; while the special-needs students demonstrated a 177% growth in word usage and a 261% growth in sentence usage over the comparison group.

    b. In Study 2, the regular education students showed a 34% increase in word usage and a 51% increase in sentence usage; while the special needs and at-risk students demonstrated a 55% increase in word usage and 112% increase in sentence usage.

2. The increase in the length of the students' writing was due to a greater increase in sentence usage rather than in word usage. Whereas the experimental group and time

period revealed a greater use of sentences, the comparison group and the comparison time period showed a greater reliance on individual word usage.

  a. Study 1: With 570 minutes of instruction, the regular-education students demonstrated an increase of 120% in word usage and 161% in sentence usage over their pre-assessment. The special-needs students demonstrated a 227% increase in word usage and a 310% increase in sentence usage over their pre-assessment.

  b. Study 2: Over an almost 4 *month* pre-assessment period, the regular-education students showed a 28% growth in word usage and a 13% growth in sentence usage. After eight *days*, but only 180 minutes of the improv sequence, they demonstrated an additional 34% increase in word usage and 51% increase in sentence usage. Over an almost 4 *month* pre-assessment period, the special-education students and at-risk students showed a 9% growth in word usage and a -6% growth in sentence usage. After only eight *days* of improv, they demonstrated an additional 55% increase in word usage and a 112% increase in sentence usage.

3. The growth in individual writing was produced after spending approximately 90% of instructional time on collaborative activities.

4. The growth in individual writing was produced after spending approximately 70% of instructional time on oral, collaborative activities.

5. Students were able to independently transfer skills gained during collaborative games and individual story writing to topic-driven journal writing without any practice or coaching.

IMPROV IMPACTS WRITING FLUENCY

Improv is a powerful and impactful intervention for increasing writing fluency, as well as other literacy skills. A student's reluctance to write may be due to social-emotional reasons or literacy-based deficits. With individual reasons usually not known to the teacher, improv serves as an effective, broad-based instructional intervention.

A. Literacy Skills: The findings from the studies, along with existing literacy research, indicate that improv provides a framework that takes students rapidly through essential literacy processes seen on the emergent level, and that exposure to and practice of these processes addresses deficits in social, emotional, or literacy skills important to writing. The sequence of games used in these studies scaffolds not only improv structures, but also scaffolds essential literacy skills that enable students to move from collaborative speech to individual writing.

B. Motivates and Engages: If a reluctance to write is because the student is not engaged in a given class or has disengaged from school entirely, improv's structure as well as the social, collaborative, and multimodal nature of improv may reengage, motivate, and deepen their learning experience.

C. Social-Emotional Skills: If a student's resistance is due to a lack of confidence in their ability or sense of worth in their own work or thoughts, then improv's collaborative nature supported by the rule *"Yes, and..."* helps by quieting self-criticism and promoting self-expression. It also creates a supportive learning environment that helps the individual develop the confidence and self-esteem needed to put their own thoughts down on paper.

A. IMPROV DEVELOPS LITERACY SKILLS

The *Improv 'n Ink* sequence is composed of four steps that enable students to address and practice literacy skills essential to the development of writing fluency.

*STEP 1: LEARNING "YES, AND..."

"Yes, and..." is the foundational rule of improv, serving both as a prompt to students to continually add their thoughts, thus increasing fluency of thought, speech, and writing. It also frames collaborative interaction, which transitions students through essential literacy processes and also develops social emotional skills. "Yes, and…" is introduced and practiced in the game, Yes, And-Planning. In this game, students work collaboratively to plan a party or item. They begin each offer by saying, "Yes, and…" out loud. In future games. "Yes, and…" becomes an internal prompt before each offer.

"YES, AND..." AS A PROMPT

Used as an external prompt in the game Yes, and-Planning, "Yes, and…" eventually serves to structure and drive a student's internal dialogue when writing. Students apply "Yes, and…" when making verbal offers and then later when making written offers. Initially, students write in collaboration, using "Yes, and…" to build off the offers of other students, moving a story forward, ultimately to resolution. Later, students use this same rule to acknowledge their own ideas, adding to them to create and resolve their own individual story. "Yes, and…" helps students when writing collaboratively and individually to increase the length of their writing by helping them add consecutive thoughts or sentences (DeMichele, 2015).

LISTENING SKILLS

"Yes, and…" supports the development of deep listening, a skill and concept used in improvisational theater, and practiced and developed through participation in improv exercises. The skill addresses the habit people have when they tend to not listen completely to what someone is saying because they are already thinking of what they will say next. In improv, new ideas are born when one presents an offer that is an elaboration of preceding offers. In order to present the best new offer, one must have fully listened to what was spoken. Listening skills are further strengthened by the practice of *Giving and Taking Attention*, which reminds students to turn their body, including eye contact and direct their physical energy when listening to an individual making an offer. This enables one to better hear and also understand the offer, while demonstrating a posture that conveys respect.

SPEAKING SKILLS

"Yes and…" necessitates that offers are communicated effectively between students. *Give and Take* fosters an awareness that one must not only give their attention so others can make an offer, but that they must effectively and respectfully take attention so they themselves can make their contribution. When an individual takes the attention to make an offer, that offer will need to be loud enough to be heard, articulate enough to be understood, and possess the appropriate tone to convey its intended meaning. The next offer will be built upon that offer and will be responsive to its words and emotional tone. Improv helps develop the individual's speaking skills by enabling them to gain an acute awareness not only of what they say and if it is loud enough, but how it is said and how that tone or intonation will influence the responding offer. The rule of "Yes, and…" and the act of taking attention is how improv gives each student a consistent opportunity to develop speaking skills.

INNER SPEECH

Students internalize "Yes, and…" while participating in collaborative improv games. By using "Yes, and…" as an internal prompt they are able to increase the length of their writing (DeMichele, 2015). Vygotsky (1978) described young children's use of external speech or self-talk in social interactions. This self-talk is eventually internalized, becoming inner speech. Moffett also believed that the development of inner speech is derived from outer speech practiced in social settings (as cited in Wagner, 1998). Transitioning from the oral use of *"Yes, and…"* in beginning collaborative improv games to the internalization of *"Yes, and…"* before speaking in more advanced improv storytelling games, allows for external speech, or "self-talk" to be gradually internalized, mirroring the progression of literacy described. [1]

*STEP 2: NARRATIVE STORYTELLING IMPROV GAMES

Before playing a storytelling game, students are introduced to basic improv story structure: establish CROW in 2-3 lines, create a problem, and then solve it. Translated, this means establish the main <u>c</u>haracters, their <u>r</u>elationships, their <u>o</u>bjectives, and the <u>w</u>here (setting). When participating in the games, students may stand or sit as a group and be allowed to act out their offer in place if they choose. Movement will help students engage, focus, and visualize (Jensen, 2001). After telling stories one word at a time, which may take 1 to 3 minutes, story games in which students contribute phrases and sentences are introduced. Those stories may take about 3 to 5 minutes and may be guided by the use of genre or story-style, which acts as a loose plot outline for different types of stories. The reinforcement of basic story elements and structure, and the use of genre prevents students from creating stories that lack sense and form and instead construct coherent narratives (Sawyer, 2002).

When following the sequence of games, approximately 70% of the time is dedicated to oral improv games. This allows students the necessary practice of essential skills and the confidence gained through oral and collaborative improv games. This structured practice will enable them to transition to collaborative writing and later to individual writing. As students collaboratively and orally create stories, they repeatedly practice thinking and speaking with "Yes, and…" as an internal prompt. The time spent playing the oral games helps the student acquire the skills to transition from thinking and speaking with "Yes, and…" to thinking and writing with "Yes, and…"

---

[1] Some of the secondary research presented on pages 46-53 also appears in:
DeMichele, M. (2015). Improv and ink: Increasing individual writing fluency with collaborative improv. *International Journal of Education and the Arts, 16*(10). Retrieved from http://www.ijea.org/v16n10/.

DEVELOPMENT OF THE NARRATIVE

Improv is an effective strategy to collaboratively create complex, well-formed, and coherent narratives. Using the concept of collaborative emergence, Sawyer (2002) explains the connection between narratives and improvisation. He contends that improvisation, with its "moment to moment, processual, contingent nature" enables children to co-create within a social and collaborative structure and allows for the emergence of narrative literacy (p. 33). Sawyer found that two elements contained in improv positively affect the development of narratives. First, improv's use of scaffolds or loose plot outlines supports the creation of coherent narratives (Sawyer, 2002). Second, studies of adult improvisational troupe performances (2003) demonstrated that when actors stepped out of their role and used out-of-character techniques, plot lines gained complexity. In Podlozny's (2000) meta-analysis of drama studies, unstructured plots facilitated oral language skills more than the structured confines of a story; however, it was also found that a combination of structured and unstructured plots, which more accurately describes improv games, were associated with larger effect size than studies using only one or the other. The writing studies showed that the structured plots were associated with larger effects. Plots were considered structured if they followed a story or script, and unstructured if they were guided by a theme. With the use of basic story structure and genres to provide a framework for the composition of stories, and with the practice of acting as narrators, which develops an awareness/sense of audience, the improv games of this sequence helps students develop well-formed, complex, and coherent narratives.

DEVELOPING ORAL SKILLS

The improv games in the core sequence offer the student the opportunity to develop oral skills, to speak ideas out loud, and to tell their collaborative stories before they pick up a pen and paper. This honors the connection between a student's development of oral and written language skills. The practice of transitioning children too quickly away from talking and to writing is detrimental to their literacy (Gillard, 1996, as cited in Simich-Dudgeon, 1998). The oral nature of drama activities, like improv, has secured it as an effective means of developing the language facility required for writing (Wagner, 1998). Yaffe (1989) used improvisation to develop writing skills by expanding on the students' oral language development. Improvisation enabled students to understand that the creation of oral scenes was essentially "writing on their feet" (p. 52).

*STEP 3: COLLABORATIVE IMPROV STORY-WRITING GAMES

During the collaborative writing activities, students sit in a group. Each student has a notebook or piece of paper. Following the same structure as the improv game they just finished, each student begins writing a story based upon the class's offer. After one word or at the teacher's command, each student passes their story to the next student in the group. It is necessary for the receiving student to read from the beginning of a story to wherever the previous student stopped writing, so that he may add the next word, phrase, or sentence(s). This passing of stories, rereading, and contributing of text is repeated during allotted time segments until the stories are finished, typically within 5 to 10 minutes depending on whether it is a one-word or multiphrase/sentence structure. At the end of the writing activity each student is in possession of the story they began, but was finished through the collaborative effort of the group.

Step 3 is essential in the transition from speaking to writing. Before students are asked to attempt individual writing, they transition from collaborative oral exercises to collaborative written exercises. This step allows students to continue developing "Yes, and…" as an internal prompt while in a fast-paced collaborative environment. Just like in the oral version of the game, students have only time to trust their peers' creative direction, think "Yes, and…" and build upon previous ideas as they move the story forward in writing. Free from the responsibility of telling the whole story and whether or not it's any good, students forget their prior reservations about writing and plunge into the collaborative writing activities with fervor. Note that students do not write about the story they created orally. Instead, each collaboratively and individually written story will be a new and spontaneous creation following a given improv game structure. This allows the student the opportunity to transition from using "Yes, and…" orally to using it as an internal prompt when writing collaboratively and then individually.

It is the power of collaboration that produces the students' ability to overcome momentary or persistent resistance to writing. Writing is a skill that is usually done in isolation by the individual student. It may even seem counterintuitive that to help a student overcome resistance to writing, they should first write in collaboration. It is exactly this approach that yields success (DeMichele, 2015). Students will spend about 70% of the time engaged in collaborative oral games and 20% of the time in collaborative written activities. They will spend only 10% of their time engaged in individual writing activities. To move past the use of collaboration too quickly is to halt the development of the literacy, collaborative, and social-emotional skills that will enable the student to have the confidence to write on their own with eagerness, abandoning their previous resistance. *Chapter 5* offers sample schedules.

TRANSITIONING FROM SPEAKING TO WRITING

Although the development of oral language supports the development of writing, transferring from one to the other is not as simple as had been previously believed (Wagner, 1998). Britton, Burgess, Martin, McLeod, and Rosen (1975) recognized the relationship between written language, inner speech, and the social nature of expressive language. Described as oral, sharing context of meaning, and feeling trust in a relation to a listener, Britton (et al. 1975) contend that expressive language "…may be the first step in the development of writing abilities"(as cited in Wagner, 1998 p.120). Transferring from oral speech to writing, however, is more complex than just speech that is written down. Moffett (quoted in Wagner, 1998) explains, "The most critical adjustment one makes [in learning to write] is to relinquish collaborative discourse, with its reciprocal prompting and cognitive cooperation, and to go it alone" (p. 118). This transition requires one to abandon the collaborative and reciprocal prompting nature of oral conversation and instead embrace a solitary environment of individual writing. Participating in collaborative, oral improv exercises that transition to collaborative, written improv and then to individual writing is *not* equivalent to talk that is written down. This scaffolded sequence of improv games addresses the complex process of transitioning from collaborative, oral language to individual, solitary writing.

A MULTIMODAL APPROACH

Improv games are multimodal by nature, embracing movement and nurturing visualization and imagination, which all impact the development of writing. Wagner (1998) cites numerous emergent literacy studies showing that "when children are making the transition from oral to written language, they give their early writing a multimodality associated with gesture and graphics" (p. 120). Improv's storytelling games allow for both gesture as well as greater movement by the students. In addition to the kinesthetic elements of improv, the constant use of imagination and creative thinking during improvisation increases one's ability to form mental images (Yau, 1989, as cited in McMaster, 1998). McKnight (2000) and Wilhelm (1997) also recognize improv's role in helping students visualize or "see text" as mental images, which consequently enhances "their ability to decipher and comprehend meaning in existing texts as well as to create expressive texts of their own through moving, speaking, and writing" (as cited in Smith & McKnight, 2009, p. 7).

READING SKILLS

While participating in the writing games, students practice fundamental reading skills that support reading fluency and comprehension. During the collaborative writing games, students repetitively reread each story: reading, scanning, visualizing, and making contextual and syntactic choices. Existing research indicates that these skills are important in the development of reading fluency and comprehension. (Bidwell, 1990; McMaster, 1998; Smith & McKnight, 2009; Wilhelm, 1997).

Fluency

In the collaborative writing activities, students in a group simultaneously write a portion of a story and then pass their story to another student. It is necessary for the receiving student to read from the beginning of a story to wherever the previous student stopped writing so that they may add on the next word, phrase, or sentence(s). This passing of stories is repeated during allotted time segments until the stories are finished. This activity is supported by reading-fluency research that emphasizes the use of repeated reading as a valuable strategy to develop reading fluency (Bidwell, 1990, as cited in McMaster, 1998). In addition to the practice of repeated reading, these collaborative writing activities aid the development of fluency by allowing students the continual practice of using contextual, semantic, and syntactic clues to compose the next word, phrase, or sentence of the story they are writing.

Comprehension

Reading comprehension skills are also practiced during these collaborative story-writing sessions. Each time a student takes their turn adding to the story they draw from prior knowledge to create meaning from text. They create visual images of what they have just read. They check for understanding and story elements so they can move the story forward with their contribution. When continuing the composition of stories they rely on inferences and synthesis. When they only have a limited amount of time left to bring a story to a resolution they must determine if all the story elements were presented, if the story arc was followed, if a genre was established, and then they compose an ending that makes sense.

Improv's consistent use of reflective and imaginative powers, which lead to a greater ability in perspective taking, mental imaging, and creative thinking, actively supports reading comprehension (Yau, 1992; as cited in McMaster, 1998).

Scanning Skills

Scanning skills are addressed at two points during the collaborative and individual writing activities. During the collaborative writing activities, students must rapidly reread each story before making contextual decisions in order to add missing story elements, further the plot line, and eventually offer resolution. Scanning skills are developed as students will be rereading possibly four or more stories numerous times before they are completed. Since students only have a minimal amount of time to add their contribution before the stories are simultaneously passed, the pressure to read quickly and to check for specific elements may develop or strengthen scanning skills. When students have finished their collaborative or individually written stories, they then identify story elements, story structure, and descriptors of genre by systematically marking their paper. When students read their marked words or phrases back to themselves or others, they are able to get a sense of the story. This helps them become aware of the information they might be looking for when scanning text.

NARRATIVE WRITING

In addition to the development of fluency skills, the *Improv 'n Ink* sequence helps teach narrative story-writing. Many supplemental resources for narrative storytelling are workbooks that use an individual and text-based approach. *Improv 'n Ink* offers a dynamic, brain-compatible, active, collaborative, and individual approach that reaches students with differing learning styles. The sequence of games quickly conveys to students the basic structure and elements of storytelling and story writing in an energetic and experiential way.

*STEP 4: INDIVIDUAL STORY WRITING

After a couple of days of collaborative story writing, students are often eager to write their own story. Individual improv story writing follows the structure of its corresponding game. Individual stories should still be based on an offer from the audience, and the time given should be about the same as in the collaborative writing version. During the sequence of games, students will spend only about 10% of the time engaged in individual improv writing. Even with this seemingly minuscule amount of time, students immediately pour out their ideas onto paper.

AUDIENCE

As they engage in individual writing, students transfer their awareness of an actual audience to a sense of audience when writing. Acting as a narrator in the oral storytelling games, students narrate to both an actual audience and also to their group members. Through their repetitive role as narrator, students transition from speaking to an audience to internalizing an awareness of audience. When engaged in individual writing, this sense of audience helps foster intention and purpose, resulting in an increase in writing length.

TRANSFERENCE

Consistent with Podlozny's (2000) findings that "drama does have the power to foster skills that then transfer to new material (p. 266)," both studies showed a clear increase in the length of writing and sentence usage over word usage for both male and female students (DeMichele, 2015). This transference occurred without any coaching or practice, as students were assessed immediately following initial exposure to the improv sequence. It is, however, still important to help students transition from collaborative, storytelling, writing assignments to individual writing. The transition to individual improv story writing is generally easy, as many students will be craving creative control at this point; however, some may benefit from a little coaching to help the transition to other individual writing assignments.

While both boys and girls in the studies wrote comparable collaborative and individual stories, the girls in both regular-education and special-education groupings showed greater increases with their individual journal writing than the boys (DeMichele, 2015). Since both boys and girls expressed comparable enthusiasm and story length during the improv writing activities, it seems that the girls transferred the skills gained to individual journal writing with greater ease than the boys. This gender gap, although based on a sample too small from which to draw firm conclusions, is supported by recent research in the Nation's Report Card: Writing (2012). This report shows female students in 8th and 12th grade writing at a higher proficiency level than boys. Education analyst Susan Pimentel, believes this difference may be explained by the test's survey in which 53% of girls agreed or strongly agreed that, "Writing is one of my favorite activities," but only 35% of the boys felt that way (Krache, 2012). Since a student's negative perception of writing may reemerge as they transition from improv story writing to non-improv writing assignments, providing multiple opportunities to revisit collaborative and individual improv writing activities should enhance a student's ability to transfer literacy and social-emotional skills to other writing assignments.

ALIGNMENT TO THE CURRICULUM

The improv games provided in this book align easily with curricula that include communication and literacy standards. Since language on state and national curricular standards are periodically revised, below is a listing of many of the individual skills that are developed through participation in these games and writing activities. Alignment to state and national standards is possible for language arts/English, as well as other academic subjects and technical classes that address literacy skills.

Communication and Collaborative Learning Skills

➢ Makes appropriate eye contact when speaking/communicating

➢ Listens actively

➢ Directs attention and focus to the person to whom they are speaking/communicating

> ➢ Builds upon ideas presented by others

> ➢ Demonstrates appropriate posture or physical actions

> ➢ Presents ideas without a fear of rejection

> ➢ Uses appropriate vocal tone and projection

> ➢ Works collaboratively

Confidence

> ➢ Commits to ideas

> ➢ Exhibits flexible and creative thinking skills

> ➢ Speaks extemporaneously

> ➢ Exhibits spontaneous thinking skills

Critique/Feedback

> ➢ Is able to explain criteria

> ➢ Offers constructive critique in the evaluation of the work of others

> ➢ Offers constructive critique in the evaluation of their own work

Story Elements

> ➢ Establishes the character, relationship, objective (plot), and where (setting) of a story

> ➢ Moves a story forward through the use of action

> ➢ Uses conflict and resolution in storytelling

> ➢ Identifies and uses different genres in their storytelling and writing

Oral and Written Language Skills

Fluency	Syntax	Synthesis	Sequencing	Prediction	Sentence structure
Inference	Context	Grammar	Vocabulary	Punctuation	

Making syntactic and contextual choices

Reading Skills

Comprehension	Fluency	Scanning Skills	Visualizing

B. IMPROV MOTIVATES AND ENGAGES

Addressed in detail in *Chapter 3,* the structure of improv produces instructional approaches that engage, reengage and motivate learners. Improv, with its collaborative, social and learner-centered structure, and its fast-paced and visual environment, is an instructional intervention capable of engaging the current generations of students (Berk & Trieber, 2009). With students engaged, improv provides them the opportunity to develop a deeper level of understanding through its constructionist approach (Sawyer, 2006). The structures not only engage, but help students develop and sustain their motivation by addressing the five basic human needs as defined by Glasser (1998): survival, belonging/connectedness, power/competence, autonomy, and fun. The honoring of students of different learning styles and intelligences through a multimodel approach (Gardner, 1993) further supports improv's ability to engage and motivate learners. Furthermore, students may find that improv honors their voice. Issues of diversity, cultural relevance, and authenticity are addressed as student offers are listened to, accepted, and validated. To summarize, the structure of improv embodies instructional strategies and approaches that successfully engage as well as reengage students with a history of failure or who have become marginalized (Smith & McKnight, 2009; Yaffe, 1989).

C. IMPROV DEVELOPS SOCIAL-EMOTIONAL SKILLS

At the core of improv is collaboration, structured and supported by the rule of "Yes, and...". It is through collaboration that social-emotional skills take root. Teachers realize that social-emotional development of their students is integral to their success in the classroom and in life. They recognize that a student's affective state directly impacts their ability to process and retain information. The affective domain, identified in Benjamin Bloom's *Taxonomy of Educational Objectives* (1956) and now supported by research in current neuroscience, is unfortunately often marginalized as teachers struggle to find the time to address these needs in the current standards-based, data-driven educational environment. Integrating improv is an efficient intervention because the development of social-emotional skills occurs by just playing the games. With no extra time or effort, teachers can teach and reinforce content while helping their students develop the social-emotional skills essential to learning.

Social-emotional skill development is produced by collaboration, framed by "Yes, and...". The implementation of "Yes, and..." teaches students to listen to a preceding idea and build upon it, not to deny it or make fun of it. With each received offer, students repeatedly ignore or work through any desire to be defensive, critical, and judgmental, or simply negating of an offer. Students working collaboratively begin to feel safe as a sense of trust develops. Students begin to trust their ability to contribute, their peers' ability to contribute, and the fact that no ideas will be rejected. Through this practice, students begin to trust peers with whom they may never have worked before, spoken to before, or even have shown any respect for prior to working in collaboration. They also begin to trust themselves, confident that they too are able make contributions worthy of acceptance by their peers, their teacher, and themselves.

This sense of trust and confidence to contribute during improv is finding validation from brain research with musical improvisation. Musical improvisation is also structured by a frame like "Yes, and...," in which one musician accepts another's offer and incrementally builds upon it before passing it back or along to another. Research involving jazz musicians shows that when improvising, the part of the brain that controls self-editing is turned off and the part of the brain associated with self-expression is active (Lopez-Gonzalez & Limb, 2012). Often, students self-judge and self-edit to such a degree that it inhibits their full participation in a lesson. The frame of "Yes, and..." practiced in improv and integrated into class activities will help students suspend overly critical judgment of themselves and peers, thereby strengthening their self-confidence and ability to work independently and with others.

The creation of a collaborative learning environment allows creativity and emotional safety to develop, not only for that instructional moment, but also for the duration of the class and school year. A collaborative environment decreases a sense of threat or anxiety an individual student might feel in the learning environment. A resulting sense of emotional safety frees students to become open and engaged in their learning, and an active member of the learning community. With a sense of threat or anxiety fading, students experience further growth in their self-esteem and self-confidence as they begin to find themselves engaged in instruction fully and with enjoyment.

During this sequence of games, the nurturing of social emotional skills occur with about 90% of instructional time dedicated to collaborative activities that practice using "Yes, and…". When participating in the games, the students are consistently practicing accepting ideas. When the students finally have the opportunity to write by themselves, they discover a level of trust, acceptance, and confidence in their own ideas that they may have not felt before. As they engage in their own individual writing, students embrace a sense of assurance that when they continue to add their own ideas one after another, those ideas will be acceptable to themselves and the teacher. *Chapter 3* addresses the development of specific social-emotional skills in further detail.

PART 2

*

GET STARTED

*

GAME SEQUENCE

*

ADDITIONAL GAMES

*

5

GETTING STARTED:

Scheduling, Design & Facilitation Strategies

Improv games are not complex or difficult. They are 3- to 5-minute games, and as explained in *Chapter 3*, there are only a four-part structure and one rule, "Yes, and," that must be followed. You will notice rather quickly that this chapter, as well as the Game Plans that follow, offer much more information than simply the directions to the game. The reason for that is the successful teaching and use of improv depends on not just knowing the games, but on how to facilitate them. This section offers ideas on scheduling, instructional design, and facilitation skills that will assist in effectively and efficiently introducing and facilitating the games.

SCHEDULING

LAYERING OF SKILLS

Games are Sequenced and Scaffolded
The core sequence games and writing activities are layered so a solid understanding of improv can be attained and desired skills can be developed and sustained by the individual and the class. Essential concepts and terminology are introduced and reinforced throughout the core sequence in a similar fashion. The following tables (Tables 5.1 and 5.2) indicate how improv and literacy skills are scaffolded within the sequence.

Scheduling of Games
The most effective way to implement this sequence of games is to find a way that integrates them into the existing classroom structure. If the students understand that these games are part of the class and not something special or separate, it will be easier for them to apply the concepts they learn to the rest of their work in the class. Initially, students will better retain the concepts and skills if the games are introduced and practiced on a daily or maybe biweekly basis. This allows

proficiency and confidence to develop at a faster pace. Caution! If the games and writing activities are presented on the same day every week, students may view that day as separate from the class, and may not clearly see the application of the concepts to the rest of their studies.

The following tables (Tables 5.3 and 5.4) show how the games might be used in a 40- to 50-minute block of time and a class size of up to 24 students. Individual games may take 3 to 5 minutes. In games like Freeze Frame and Freeze Tag, students take turns entering the game. These turns may take less than a minute. It may be beneficial to review games on the following day.

Table 5.1 Core Sequence: Layering of Skills

Game	"Yes and…"	Story Elements	3-Step Story Structure	C W	I W
#1 Yes and-	Say Aloud -Apply verbally	C: not applicable R: not applicable O: audience W: not applicable			
#2 We Are	Think -Apply verbally	C: given R: given O: student W: audience	One-word story approx. three lines in length.		
#3 Volley Word	Think -Apply verbally -Apply in CW	C: audience R: student O: student W: student	One-word story approx. five lines in length.	X	
#4 Did You Hear the One About…?	Think -Apply verbally -Apply in CW -Apply in IW	C: audience R: student O: student W: student Genre: teacher (optional)	Story offers are phrases and sentences; the length is determined by the teacher or time limit.	X	X
#5 Story-Story!	Think -Apply verbally -Apply in CW -Apply in IW	C: student R: student O: student W: student Genre: audience	Story offers are phrases and sentences; the length is determined by the teacher or time limit.	X	X

CW: Collaborative Writing IW: Individual Writing C: Character R: Relationship O: Objective W: Where

Table 5.2 Core Sequence: Overview and Comparison of Skills

CORE GAMES	Communication Skills	Story Elements	Writing & Reading	Movement Required	Stage & Drama Techniques
#1 Yes, And-	X				
#2 We Are	X	X		O	
#3 Volley Word*	X	X	X		
#4 Did you hear?*	X	X	X	O	
#5 Story-Story!*	X	X	X	O	
ADDITIONAL					
Zip-Zap-Zop!	X			X	
Yes and...flow	X			X	
Freeze Frame	X	X		X	X
Freeze Tag	X	X		X	X

*Includes oral and writing games. O: Optional movement done in place.

Table 5.3 Schedule with Core Games

DAY	GAMES	POSSIBLE SCHEDULE
1	"Yes and..."	20–25 min: Improv. Game
2	We Are	15–30 min: Improv. Game
3	Volley Word	15–30 min: Improv. Game 10–15 min: Collaborative Writing
4	Did You Hear The One About...?	10–15 min: Improv. Game 10–15 min: Collaborative Writing 10–15 min: Individual Writing
5	Story-Story!	10–15 min: Improv. Game 10–15 min: Collaborative Writing 10–15 min: Individual Writing

*Although Zip-Zap-Zop is in the Additional Game section because it requires movement, the movement is done in place with all the students standing/sitting in a circle. If possible, use as a daily warm-up.

Table 5.4 Integrate Additional Games

GAME	OVERVIEW	TIME TO INTRODUCE	GAME LENGTH
Zip-Zap-Zop!	Serves as a warm-up. Builds communication skills.	Before Yes...And Planning.	5 min.
"Yes, and...Flow"	Supports understanding of *"Yes, and..."* through movement.	After or before Yes...And Planning.	5–10 min.
Freeze Frame	Practices the establishment of CROW while creating a scene.	After Volley Word	10–20 min.
Freeze Tag	Practices the establishment of CROW while creating a scene.	After Did You Hear the One About...?	10–20 min.

TRANSFERENCE OF SKILLS TO OTHER WRITING ASSIGNMENTS

After completing the sequence of games, including writing activities, help students transfer fluency skills to other writing assignments. Start first with journal entries or a type of free writing assignment. Formal essays or content-based responses should be introduced after free writing assignments. Remember that some students may transfer skills with greater ease then others, so on a day with a writing assignment consider starting class with a quick collaborative storytelling game and even an individual improv story-writing activity to help students transfer their fluency to a more structured assignment.

INSTRUCTIONAL DESIGN

The process of learning to mastery is the same for children, adolescents, and adults of diverse learning styles. The Game Plans follow a four-step instructional design framework, based upon the work of Dr. Bernice McCarthy (2006), which honors different learning styles while teaching to mastery. This four-step framework helps ensure a successful implementation by organizing the essential elements of teaching improv for the purpose of addressing writing fluency.

1. **Create Relevance:** Discuss with the class or guide them through an activity that will help them understand why playing the given improv game is relevant to their lives. Some games reinforce the concepts introduced in preceding games; therefore, the teacher may not need to create relevance for each game.

Creating relevance helps a student understand why a game is relevant to their lives. It should not be assumed that students will just eagerly jump at the opportunity to "play games." If students understand the educational and personal relevance of these games, they will be more willing to engage and acquire the intended skills.

Teacher resistance is often blamed for why improv is not used more extensively in classrooms. In some instances, however, the greater obstacle to introducing improv is resistance from the students. How a teacher creates relevance for a game is critical for successful implementation. It is not uncommon to hear, "I'm too tired." "Why are we playing games?" "I'm here to learn." "I have other work to do." "This is stupid." As children may be more willing to just jump in and play games, adolescents and adults may not. It is therefore essential to create relevance for all populations before actually implementing the game.

Another important reason to create relevance is because students must also accept that when directing improv, their teacher will move from an authoritarian role to a more guiding or coaching role. Often, it is not the teacher but the students who need help in understanding this shift. It is not uncommon to hear the following: "It's the teacher's job to control us." "Why are you not in front of the class?" "Hey, you're in charge, why are you sitting in the audience?" This paradigm held by students can be very ingrained, necessitating that improv games be framed and implemented purposefully and with care.

When "Create Relevance" is offered in the instructions of a game, it is presented in a scripted format. It is simply what I found worked for me. Feel free to create your own. I used a simple discussion format because it was quick, effective, and allowed me to move to the game in a few minutes. Possibilities are limitless, especially if you have the instructional time to use multi-media approaches. Relevance does not need to be created for each game, as some games are a variation of the previous game and their "Focus" topics are the same.

2. **Introduce New Information:** Introduce the Game or Writing Activity. Coach a small group of students through the game, so they model it for all. Detailed directions on how to facilitate the games are provided in the "Game Plans" of each game.

3. **Practice:**

   a. **Practice:** Allow everyone to play the Game/Activity.

   b. **Acknowledgment of the Effort/Gratitude:** Acknowledgment/gratitude is given by the audience to the players and from the players to the audience after the completion of each game.

   c. **Feedback:** After each group of students has played, a short and focused feedback session occurs. Feedback should stay focused on the topics listed in the "Focus" section on the top of the game plan. Language suggestions for the feedback session are given in this chapter. When modeled by the teacher, this language will help students learn appropriate and productive ways to give specific feedback to themselves and others. Feedback is a regular and essential part of improv instruction. Please see *Chapter 3* for further explanation of feedback as part of the improv's structure and its role in increasing engagement, motivation, and learning.

   d. **Rubrics:** The provided rubrics break down the topics in the "Focus" section in more detail and may be useful to guide feedback sessions when students are more comfortable with giving feedback. The rubrics offered in this book are not designed to create summative numerical grades for performances. They instead serve the facilitator and the students as a visual tool to help them focus on basic improv rules and essential skills for each individual game. The rubrics enable the students to see how the games are scaffolded, understand expectations, and monitor progress. The skills in the rubrics are a more specific breakdown of the rules and concepts targeted in the "Focus" section of the Game Plan. The rubric can be useful when:

➤ Creating surveys for students to self-assess their comfort with skills

➤ Given to students as a tool for self and peer assessment

➤ Used as a pre- and post-assessment tool to track students' skill development

4. Adaptations and Integrations: Adapting the games into writing activities and integrating content into the game structures will help students transfer developed skills to other classroom writing assignments. Types of integrations and adaptations offered include:

➤ Collaborative story writing

➤ Individual story writing

➤ Content integration: ideas for how curricular content can be integrated into the games

FACILITATION STRATEGIES

What is not usually presented in workshop trainings or written resources regarding using improv in the classroom are facilitation strategies that can really make a difference in the overall success of the games. Please understand that any language selections presented in this section or in the "Game Plans" are suggested, not scripted. The language offered in "Giving and Receiving Feedback" and "Acknowledgment" is frequently used by teachers of theater in which feedback and acknowledgment is given after each and every student performance. The language and techniques in "Giving Effective Directions" are used commonly by teachers who direct students in movement-based activities. Teachers of physical education, marching band, sports, performing arts, and vocational classes may find these techniques familiar.

GIVING AND RECEIVING FEEDBACK
Within the structure of all improv games is the opportunity to offer feedback, whether that involves the group offering its critique or an individual silently assessing what worked and what did not work. With each improv game, individuals learn and practice giving effective feedback and receiving productive feedback. The overall tone of the group becomes one of support. Feelings of personal attacks and rants of defensiveness begin to disappear as giving and receiving feedback is routinely practiced.

Teachers: Giving and Receiving Feedback

Teachers will use feedback to help students develop an awareness of the skills that are being targeted. The improv skills developed are given in the "Focus" section of a Game Plan. By focusing on these, the skills under "Goals/Objectives," which are outlined in the rubric for that game, will develop. It may be tempting to discuss other skills present in a game; however, if focus is given to just the improv skills, the students will gain competency, confidence, and acquire skills at a much quicker rate. Although the rubric will give detail to the discussion, feedback should remain focused on the topics in the "Focus" section.

Language Choice: Appropriate language orientation is vital to effective side coaching. The correct choice in wording will foster a productive and supportive relationship within the class. To decrease the threatening perception of feedback, and especially feedback in front of peers, use the following language orientation. When giving feedback to the students, try to refrain from phrasing thoughts with I and you; instead use words such as we, our, and let's, or omit pronouns entirely (Allen, 2002, p. 143). For example, try to avoid saying, "You did not establish an objective." "Did they establish an objective?" Instead try, "Was an objective established?" "An objective was not established." "Let's work on establishing an objective next time."

This change in language orientation can remove the inherent threat of receiving feedback, or as many students still perceive it, "criticism," or "being yelled at." The feedback in the first example is often perceived as a personal attack by an authority figure and usually elicits some degree of a defensive response from the individual receiving the feedback. The language choice demonstrated in the second example instead conveys a sense of "team" to the student. The teacher chooses language that is supportive and conveys a sense of unity in effort as everyone reaches for the same goals together.

Students: Giving and Receiving Feedback

Critiquing Others: Students should also focus their observation on the targeted skill and be encouraged to model the teacher's use of language when giving feedback. This will create a friendly and more comfortable rapport between students since they are not personally critiqued, but only their performances or elements of their stories.

Critiquing Themselves: If students are asked to critique themselves, ask them only to evaluate their comfort or mastery of the few skills for the given activity. This may avoid students feeling overwhelmed and crumbling into self-deprecation and ultimately resistance.

Response to Feedback: Students who receive feedback in this manner will be less inclined to display resistant attitudes or launch into lengthy defensive explanations. When questions are asked about whether an essential skill or element was presented, a simple "yes" or "no," and a final "thank you" would be an appropriate response. If students do follow up with questions they will tend to be ones which that clarify uncertainties they may have about skills and concepts, thus presenting the teacher with valuable, teachable moments.

ACKNOWLEDGMENT OF EFFORT/GRATITUDE

A step to acknowledging effort is included in the directions of each game. Although this will be routine to some, it is not to others. I have seen instructors at the end of a group's performance simply say, "OK, take your seats. Next group." Acknowledging and showing gratitude toward an individual's or group's effort is an essential communication and interpersonal skill. In this day of technology, the simple act of applauding for a live performance cannot be taken for granted. At live performances, performers grow frustrated at crowds that seem unwilling to stop recording on personal devices and enjoy and respond to the performance. More adults seem oblivious to their role to applaud or somehow acknowledge when musicians who perform live at a club, café, or elsewhere end a song or a set. In schools, it is no longer surprising when entire classes of students sit silent at the end of a live performance, requiring instructions from teachers that they should applaud.

Acknowledging effort and showing gratitude can positively impact the performance of an individual or group. The short nature of improv activities grants the teacher, the students and the audience many repeated opportunities to acknowledge and show gratitude for one anothers' efforts. This reciprocal form of acknowledgment is effective in lifting the spirits of individual students, encouraging involvement, signaling the completion of the activity, and as a means of continuing to build the cohesiveness of the class. After an activity or a period of feedback a simple, "Thank you. Give them a hand," or "Give yourselves a hand," inviting applause, signals the completion of the task while giving acknowledgment and showing gratitude for everyone's efforts. Invite the students in the audience to applaud the students who performed, and the performing students to applaud their audience. The audience is involved in each game through their "offers" and will appreciate being acknowledged.

GIVING EFFECTIVE DIRECTIONS

Sometimes teachers are hesitant to integrate improv because they feel that it might take too much time to get the class moving and on task. We have all wondered at some point as to, "How am I going to get them to move from here to there without bedlam breaking out?" Student cries of "What do we do now?" can be frustrating. When using interactive activities or activities that involve movement, giving directions clearly and concisely is essential for the successful engagement of the class and completion of the lesson. The following suggested strategies on giving directions to increase student involvement, decrease management issues, and increase time on task are borrowed from Dr. Rich Allen (2010).

One at a Time

Give only one direction at a time. When more than one direction is given, students may feel uncertain about one or more of the steps. When students are uncertain they may repeatedly ask "What do we do now?" or they may simply resist participating for fear of looking "dumb." Giving one direction at a time allows the student to succeed at each step (Allen, 2010, p. 49). Although the teacher will wait for the students to complete each direction before giving the next, the teacher will need to provide the energy and pace to keep students moving along efficiently.

For example:

1.   Please stand up. (teacher waits)

2.   Make one line that starts next to the map and extends to the door. (teacher waits)

3.   Now turn and face the windows. (teacher waits)

Directionalize

Notice in the above directions, the terms left and right were not used. Left and right can be confusing to some students and class debate will erupt immediately on whether you meant your right or their right. To eliminate confusion and therefore save valuable time, use hand gestures to indicate where students should be and where they should be directing their attention. You might also use physical objects in the classroom to help students position themselves, as seen in the previous example (Allen, 2010, pp. 53-54).

Congruence

Congruence refers to communicating directions with your entire self in order to increase student understanding and participation (Allen, 2010, p. 53).

➤   Make sure all students can see you when you give directions. Do not give directions if students are sitting with their backs to you. Make sure they turn around before you give a direction.

➤   Make eye contact with the students.

➤   Use physical gestures to help direct the students where to move.

➤   Use a firm tone of voice.

Four-Part Sequence

Sometimes students feel a sense of threat or anxiety when they are unsure of when to begin a given direction. We've all seen students jump to do what the teacher just said before the teacher was finished giving the direction. That can waste time and lead to management issues as the teacher struggles to regain their focus. The Four-Part Sequence makes it very clear to a student when to begin a direction (Allen, 2010, pp. 54-56).

1.   In 10 seconds…

2.   When I say, *"Go"*

3.   Give a direction.

4.   *"Go!"*

Keep It Concise

Notice from the two examples given that very few words are used in each step. Keeping directions concise will help students focus on the most important words and enable them to follow the directions quickly and accurately (Allen, 2010, pp. 45-45, 50-51). Sometimes teachers tend to add extraneous phrases before a direction. They might say, "What I'd like you to do is…" or "OK, everybody, this is what we are going to do…" Students will tend to tune out those extra words and the directions along with them. Keep directions concise to ensure efficiency. For example, instead of saying, "OK, everyone, what I want you to do now is to stand up and make a circle." Instead, simple say, "Please stand up and make a circle."

Step Check

Step check is a way to check if each student has completed a given direction or is at the same point in the activity. When the teacher confirms that the students are at the same point, then the next direction or portion of information should be given (Allen, 2010, p. 52). Step check also keeps the class' progression on each task together, thus eliminating potential management issues that sometime arise when some students get too far behind and some too far ahead. For example, using this technique will be crucial when guiding the class through the collaborative writing activities. Groups of students will be eager to begin on their own, so giving the preliminary directions step by step and checking that the class is together will lead to a successful story-writing session.

Example:

1.   Please open your own notebook. (direction)

2.   Write the names of everyone in your group on the top of the page. (direction)

3.   If you have everyone's name down, raise your pen in the air. (step check)

4.   Great, this is a story about a … (class gives an offer)… aardvark.

5.   Underneath the names, in the center of the page, write, "Aardvark." (direction)

6.   Everyone look at one anothers' page and if everyone's page is set up correctly, raise your hands. (step-check)

7.   Great! Begin writing. (direction)

Language Choice

Making intentional and deliberate choices regarding language when facilitating these games and activities can increase the effectiveness and efficiency of each activity.

➢ *When Giving Directions:* Often teachers start a direction with a phrase like, "I want you to…," and then they give the direction. This can create a power play with some students. Instead of focusing on the direction, their focus is on "this is something the teacher wants me to do." Instead of saying, "I want you to…" just give the direction as described in *Keep it Concise.*

➢ *During Collaborative Writing Activities:* Students will be told by the teacher to stop writing and pass their story to the next student. This can feel jolting to the student. It might cause stress, panic and ultimately resistance to the direction as students try to finish their thoughts. To avoid this and to keep momentum going, instead of just saying, "Stop. Pass your paper." try saying, "Whereever you are is fine. Please pass your paper." (Allen, 2010, p. 72).

➢ *During Individual Writing Activities:* These activities are designed to be completed during class time. When some students become aware of a time limit, they may panic and allow the resulting stress to shut down their ability to write to their ability. Use the technique described in the previous step. Instead of saying to the student, "You only have 5 minutes left," try saying, "You still have 5 minutes."

APPROPRIATE MATERIAL

Using improvisational activities in the classroom are highly beneficial in so many ways; however, students on occasion introduce language or topics that are not appropriate in a given classroom. Set clear parameters stating what language and topics are and are not appropriate. If a student brings up an inappropriate subject or uses offensive language it may be because:

- ➢ They are doing it for the attention and to get a reaction from the teacher and their peers.
- ➢ They do not know what is and is not appropriate language or topics for that class.
- ➢ The student blurted out the first thing that came to their mind, and unfortunately they might be at an age when their minds are being influenced by surging hormones.
- ➢ In response to the first and second scenario, let the students know before activities begin what will be considered appropriate or inappropriate language and topics. Words that are considered vulgar in schools are acceptable on television, radio, and other settings familiar to students. Some topics and language may be acceptable in the curriculum of other classes, but may not be appropriate in your class. After an initial discussion of what is inappropriate, a quick reminder of "Remember to keep it G rated" helps students remember what language and behavior is acceptable. Improv can be a wonderful teaching tool to discuss appropriateness of language and topics in certain settings and for certain audiences.
- ➢ Although some teachers might choose to allow topics such as drug use, sex, teen pregnancy, violence, and other possibly controversial topics as acceptable material for use in the games, these topics are *not* necessary to reap the benefits of the games and activities. When these topics are specifically not an option, creativity is unleashed. Being free of rehashing what they might be bombarded with every day, students sometimes surprise themselves and teachers by creating fun and amazing stories.

In any case, if a student brings up an inappropriate topic or uses vulgar language, try to assess whether it was intentional. If the student committed the infraction out of ignorance of what is appropriate or they accidentally slipped, simply reprimanding them may leave them confused and resistant to engaging in the activity in the future. Instead, educate them as to what is acceptable and help them develop an internal sensor. Whatever the reason for the use of inappropriate language or topics, stop the game immediately and address the issue.

PHYSICAL CONTACT

With the exception of the option of hooking arms in the game, We Are, the five core games do not involve or invite the opportunity for any physical contact. Only the games of Freeze Frame and Freeze Tag in the Additional Game section in *Chapter 7* may involve physical contact. Five rules for physical contact are given in that section. Pretend and slow-motion physical fighting are also discussed and not allowed for the simple reason that it is a form of denial and is, of course, not safe.

6

THE IMPROV 'N INK SEQUENCE:

The Five Core Games

BEFORE YOU BEGIN...

These five games must be presented in sequence. Each game either introduces improv and literacy skills and concepts or reinforces them from the previous game. Each game is introduced in great detail with an overview, game example, new terms and concepts, instructions, a game example with coaching, additional notes, and instructions on how to adapt the game for writing or integrate the game with course content. Although detailed, the improv games are not complicated. As described in *Chapter 3*, adherence to *one rule* and a *four-part structure* will achieve intended skill development, engagement, and motivation. This detailed and convenient layout helps to ensure that implementation goes smoothly and the intended results are achieved.

SEQUENCE OF GAMES

In the scheduling section of *Chapter 5*, the scaffolding of literacy skills is presented. The sequence also scaffolds improv skills so both teachers and students learn the games with confidence. Games are often described as easy or hard. What generally increases the level of difficulty in a game is how many and what kind of skills are required. The following table (Table 6.1) shows which concepts or skills are required for each game. Although Yes, and-Planning introduces a great number of improv skills, it is one of the easiest to play and facilitate. The difficulty level really increases with the addition of scene-based games, which require additional drama skills like staging, endowment, movement, etc. These games are contained in *Chapter 7*. Additional games are optional, and may be integrated into the sequence when the teacher and students are ready. To avoid issues that arise when the games are too complex, as described in *Chapter 3*, always follow the first step of the four-step improv structure, "The teacher/director chooses the game." Taking the time to create a firm foundational understanding will help both the teacher and students to appreciate, enjoy and benefit from the simplicity and power of the games.

Table 6.1 Scaffolding of Improv Skills

NEW TERMS and TOPICS Core Games and Additional Games	#1 Yes, And-	#2 We Are	#3 Volley Word	#4 Did You Hear	#5 Story-Story!	Zip-Zap-Zop	Yes, And-Flow	Freeze Frame	Freeze Tag
Yes, And	*	~	~	~	~		~	~	~
Give and Take	*	~	~	~	~		~	~	~
Audience	*	~	~	~	~		~	~	~
Offer	*	~	~	~	~		~	~	~
Denial	*	~	~	~	~		~	~	~
CROW		*	~	~	~		~	~	~
Move Forward with Action		*	~	~	~			~	~
End a Sentence		*	~	~	~				
Genre/Story-Style				~	*			~	~
Asking Questions								*	~
Basic Staging								*	~
Endowment								*	~
Physical Contact								*	~

*Introduce skills; ~ Reinforce skills

REVIEW OF GAME SECTION LAYOUT:

Depending upon the nature of the game and whether it is introducing or reinforcing specific skills, Game Plans will contain all or some of the following topics:

- ► Game Overview
- ► Game Example
- ► New Terms and Topics
- ► Game Plan
- ► Coaching and Notes
- ► Adaptations and Integrations

GAME PLAN OVERVIEW

The instructions to the improv games and writing activities are given in an instructional design framework that is described in *Chapter 5*. The game instructions (Game Plan) contain steps that will be repeated in detail for each game. Although seemingly redundant, this approach was taken for the following reasons. First, some will be learning improv for the first time, and by having each set of instructions complete, teachers will not have to flip back to previous games to be reminded how to do a certain step. Also, it is to help teachers facilitate improv games correctly. In my experience, I have seen many enthusiastic teachers both new to and familiar with improv make seemingly minor changes to the rules and structure of the game with catastrophic results. As described in *Chapter 3*, compromising the rules and structures of improv by ignoring "Yes, and...", or by not taking the time to allow acknowledgment or feedback, for example, will greatly inhibit improv's delivery of skills development, motivation, and engagement.

It is crucial to not have a group demonstrate the game and then allow the other groups to play at the desks at the same time. This will not allow for real-time coaching by the teacher to ensure that rules and structures are practiced correctly by each student. It will also eliminate the feedback phase of the structure, which helps all students better understand the expectations and assessment of the performance. By not taking the time to have each group perform the improv game in front of the class, the development of skills, engagement, motivation, and learning will be diminished. There is also the potential for noise and management issues to arise. If time is the concern, short-form improv games, including feedback, should take no more than 3 to 4 minutes per group.

The improv writing activities will be done at desks in groups all at the same time. The students at this time are familiar with the structure and the rules of a given game. Student progress and engagement are also easily monitored by the teacher, as pairs or groups of students silently pass their notebooks to one another at the teacher's command.

Four-Part Instructional Design *(Discussed in Chapter 5, pp. 60-62)*

1. *Create Relevance*: To help students understand the personal relevance of participating in a game, ideas and suggestions are offered in some games. Feel free to develop your own.

2. *Introduce Game*: Instead of lecturing or explaining how the game will be played, simply have a few volunteers model how the game is played with the help of the teacher coaching them through it. This will avoid confusion and resistance caused by a long series of directions or because the game "sounds stupid."

3. *Practice*: In addition to being engaged as the audience, all students actively participate in each game. Review *Chapter 5* for facilitation strategies that may be useful.

4. *Apply*: The game is then adapted to be a writing activity or integrated with course content so that students can better transfer skills developed during the games to their writing and other course work.

Four-Step Improv Structure *(Discussed in Chapter 3, pp. 34-35)*

Embedded within the *four-part instructional design model* that frames the instructions or Game Plan for each game is the *four-step improv structure*. As discussed in *Chapter 3*, this structure is responsible for increasing student motivation by meeting the five basic human needs as defined by

Glasser (1998.) By following this structure, desired skills and an increase in engagement, motivation and deepening of learning can develop.

1. The teacher chooses a game. This step is not stated but implied in each *Game Plan*. In addition, the games are in a specific sequence, so choice is not an issue unless choosing to integrate the additional games.

2. The audience makes an offer. This is stated in each *Introduce Game* section of the Game Plan.

3. The *Practice* section in each Game Plan ensures that all students have the opportunity to practice each game.

4. *Feedback* is included in the *Practice* section and is given after each group of students finishes a game. *Chapter 3* discusses the importance of this step for motivation, engagement, and skill development, while *Chapter 5* offers strategies on how to facilitate feedback sessions.

YES, AND-PLANNING

$#1$

Yes, And-Planning introduces students to the foundational improv rule of "Yes, and...". This game provides the necessary and focused practice on using "Yes, and," which is essential for the success of all improv games. This game also introduces the skill of *giving and taking attention*. Students work in expandable collaborative groups with the goal of verbally planning an activity or item in collaboration with group members. This game is low threat since students may begin planning in groups of three with their friends. Within a single session, the game provides a structure for the entire class to work collaboratively, building cohesiveness and an emotionally safe environment.

* Students practice "Yes, and..." as an external prompt.

* Students begin to develop collaborative skills that will in turn lead to the development of the many social-emotional, performance, and literacy skills described in *Chapters 3 and 4*.

* Students learn that they have the power to not give their attention to disruptive students and in turn take the teacher's attention back. Students who might be regularly disruptive quickly learn that the attention they seek is attained when they follow the rules of improv.

* Game structure can be used to review curricular content and for brainstorming.

GAME EXAMPLE

Three students stand side by side in front of the class. Although standing is recommended, students could sit in a group of three to play this game. They should all face the class so the class can better hear their offers.

Example 1:

Teacher: What kind of party do you want these people to plan?
Audience: A birthday party for a dog!
Student A: Hey, let's plan a birthday party for a dog.
Student B: Yes, and the cake could be shaped like a bone.
Student C: Yes, and we could have a cat piñata.
Student B: Yes, and the piñata could be filled with doggy treats.

Yes, And-Planning | **73**

Student A: Yes, and each dog could get fire hydrants as party favors.

Teacher: Great! Thank you! Give them a hand! (Teacher, performers, and audience claps for on another.)

Example 2:

Teacher: What item would you like them to plan?

Audience: A new car!

Student A: Hey, let's plan a new car.

Student B: Yes, the car could be painted red.

Student C: Yes, it could have orange flames painted on it.

Student B: Yes, and it could go really, really fast.

Student A: Yes, and it could have rockets.

Student C: Yes, and it could fly.

Student A: Yes, and it could turn invisible.

Teacher: Great! Thank you! Give 'em a hand!

NEW TERMS & TOPICS

YES, AND...!

The foundation of improv is "Yes, and..." With this simple phrase, an idea, when acknowledged, builds and further expands. The game, Yes, and-Planning, teaches students to build upon the preceding offer. The side coaching to "Yes, and..." reminds them to do so. "Yes, and..." is the power behind the success of each improv activity and is responsible for the acquisition of most of the skills and attributes attainable through improv.

GIVING and TAKING ATTENTION

Giving and Taking Attention is an essential skill for collaborative groups. So often by design or default, individuals find themselves placed in groups with dominant personalities who contribute most of the ideas, while others sit quietly. "Giving attention" means that the individual "gives attention" to another so they may "offer" an idea. A student "gives attention" by stopping their speaking, and directing their physical energy and eye contact to another student. This action may be challenging to some who are accustomed to coming up with all the ideas in a group setting. "Taking attention" means that an individual actively "takes the attention" from another. In order to "take the attention" from another, the student needs to speak with conviction and loudly enough to be heard, so that others stop speaking and turn their attention to the student attempting to "take the attention" from them. This skill may be quite effortless for some, but challenging for the more introverted or for individuals whose ideas are commonly ignored or dismissed.

ROLE OF THE AUDIENCE/CLASS

Individuals who are not participating will act as the audience. The audience or rest of the group is involved in the activities by giving "offers." This will help avoid management issues in two ways. First, the "audience" is actively engaged in the games from the start and not a passive observer. Second, "exhibitionism withers away when players see members of the audience not as judges or censors or even as delighted friends but as a group with whom experience is being shared. (Spolin, 2011, p. 56)."

AN OFFER

An "offer" refers to the idea that a student offers or contributes to a scene or story. The games and writing activities described in this book require offers from the participating individuals or from the individuals who are acting as the audience. The example illustrates how "offers" are used in improv. In the game Yes, And…Planning, students who are actively planning and the audience are asked to "offer" their ideas in this exercise.

Example:

Teacher:	What kind of party do you want these three people to plan?
Class Offer:	A birthday party for a dog!
Student A's Offer:	Let's plan a birthday party for a dog!
Student B's Offer:	Yes, and we could get a cake shaped like a dog bone!

DENIAL

A "denial" is a denial of the absolute foundation of improv, *"Yes, and…"* When a student denies another student's offer, it is as if the breaks were slammed on the creative process. Momentum stops. The scene or game is halted. The following examples illustrate how denials may arise.

Example 1: Saying "No…" or "Yes, but…"
The student begins their offer with "No" or "Yes, but," and continues to negate the prior offer.

Student A:	Yes, and the doll could be really big.
Student B:	No, it could be really small.
	Yes, but it could be really small.

Example 2: Negating the offer

The student says "Yes," but then offers an idea completely unrelated to the prior offer, thus negating it.

Student A: Yes, and let's go to the movies
Student B: Yes, and we could go skiing.

Example 3: Fighting

This denial will be common in scene-based games, such as Freeze Frame and Freeze Tag in *Chapter 7*. Some students try to move a scene forward by starting a fight with denials. For instance, when the fighting format of, "Yes, it is" No, it isn't." "Yes." "No." "Yes." "No." is used; no action or new information is added. No new ideas are offered. The story or scene stops.

Example 4: Killing Off Main Characters

Another way denial occurs is when a student kills off a main character. This will be common in the storytelling games. Students will sometimes kill off the main character during the beginning or middle of a story in an attempt to replace that character with one they prefer to simply end the game.

Why Denials Happen

- ✓ The student did not hear or listen to a prior "offer."

- ✓ The student is accustomed to being in creative control.

- ✓ The student seeks to create a quick laugh from others by "denying" in a way that makes fun of the preceding idea. This is done at the expense of the other student(s) and of the game.

*When a "denial" occurs, remind the student to "Yes...and." Denials are important teaching moments for the players and the audience.

GAME PLAN

FOCUS: 1. Giving and Taking Attention 2. Yes, and..."	GOALS: See Rubric STUDENT POSITIONING: Minimal space in front of class Standing circle around classroom

DIRECTIONS:

Create Relevance

When working with others, everyone needs to give and take.

New ideas are often created by adding to an existing idea.

Below is a guided question framework that may help students gain an awareness of how collaborative group work can be enjoyable and productive when all students respectfully acknowledge on another ideas and expand upon them. Relevance can also be created by helping students realize that frustrations experienced when working in groups are experienced by everyone.

» Have you ever worked in a group? Did you ever notice that sometimes one person seems to come up with all the ideas or all the answers? Or have you been in a group where there is someone who doesn't seem to contribute much or even anything? Well, actually neither scenario is really any fun for anybody because the person who comes up with all the ideas might feel like, "Why do I have to do everything?" The people who don't seem to do anything might be thinking, "No one ever listens to me anyway. Why should I bother saying or doing anything?"

» Students are also sometimes interested to find out that various professions frequently use collaborative groups that use the "Yes, and..." rule when creating new products, movies, video games, technology, etc.

» What are some of your favorite sitcoms, TV shows, movies, cartoons, etc.? Have you ever played a video game and thought how cool it would be to design one? Often, ideas for these are created by people working in collaboration, who are either trained in or are using the rules and structures of improv.

» This next activity can help make working in groups more enjoyable and effective

Introduce Game

1. *Demonstrate:* Follow steps 2-9.

2. The game begins with three volunteers standing side by side in front of the class. A group size of three ensures that all students feel the need to give and take attention. Groups can be expanded after all have participated in groups of three.

3. *Audience Offer:* Ask the audience what kind of party or type of item they want the three students to design. For example, the class gives an offer of a "birthday party."

4. Direct the three to think of things you might find or do at a "birthday party."

5. One starts and says... "Hey, let's plan a "birthday party!"

6. Another takes the attention and offers an idea starting with the phrase, "Yes, and..." For example: "Yes, and...we could have a cake."

7. The other then takes the attention and gives another offer beginning with "Yes, and..." For example: "Yes, and....it could have pink icing."

8. Allow students to take sequential turns so they get comfortable making offers beginning with "Yes, and...". When comfortable, the students should randomly offer their ideas. This practices giving and taking attention while working collaboratively with others.

9. Denials will occur during demonstrations. Be sure to immediately correct any denial with a simple reminder to use "Yes, and...".

10. *End with acknowledgment:* This game continues until the teacher says "Thank you! Give them a hand!" Allow applause. The teacher and students positively acknowledge one anothers' efforts.

Practice

11. Repeat steps 2-12 until all students have had an opportunity to participate in front of the class.

12. *Feedback:* Discuss whether the topics in the "Focus" section were achieved. Did the group "Yes, and...?" Did they build off one anothers' ideas? Did they stay focused on planning the party? Was attention given? Was attention taken? See Giving and Receiving Feedback in *Chapter 5*. The rubric (optional) can provide additional detail to the discussion and/or serve as a self, group, or teacher assessment.

Apply

13. After all have participated, start with three students in front of the class and begin a Planning Party. After they have made a few offers, add a few individuals at a time until you have the entire class planning together. This can be a very powerful moment in creating a collaborative environment for future classroom activities. It also encourages the participation of students who resisted being in a group of three in front of the class. A type of school dance or holiday party works well. Follow steps 9-12.

14. *Transference:* After all students have participated, integrate the structure of Yes, and-Planning into content instruction and reviews. Examples are contained in "Adaptations and Integrations" at the end of this section.

COACHING & NOTES

COACHING:

Teacher:	**What type of party would you like them to plan?**
Audience:	A birthday party for a dog!
Student A:	Hey, let's plan a birthday party for a dog.
Student B:	Yes, and we could have a cake.
Student C:	Yes, and we could have decorations.
Teacher:	**Have big ideas. Remember it's a birthday party for a dog.**
Student B:	The cake could be shaped like a bone.
Teacher:	**Yes, and...**
Student B:	Yes, and the cake could be shaped like a bone.
Student A:	Yes, and the cake could have icing with spots like a Dalmatian.

Student C:	Yes, and the icing could glow in the dark.
Student A:	Yes, and we could paint our faces with it.
Teacher:	**Remember it's about the party, not the icing.** *(If students begin to go too long on a tangent, remind them to refocus on what they are supposed to be planning.)*
Student C:	Yes, and we could play pin the tail on the cat.
Student A:	No. We can play pin the tail on the mailman.
Teacher:	**Denial. Remember to "Yes, and..." Yes, and...we could play pin the tail on the cat.**
Student B:	Yes, and we could have a piñata.
Student A:	Yes, and it could be shaped like a mailman.
Student B:	Yes, and it could be filled with doggy treats.
Student C:	Yes, and each dog could get mini fire hydrants as party favors.
Teacher:	**Great! Thank you! Give them a hand!** *(Both participants and audience clap for one another.)*

TEACHER'S NOTES:

Planning Suggestions:

School/Community Party, Birthday Party, Party for a Pet, School Dances	Fundraisers, Doll, Toy, Video Game, Bike, Car, Type of Product, Tech Product

*Important: Do not plan a movie or story. The storytelling games that follow Yes, And-Planning will teach students how to properly construct stories.

Remind Students to:

✓ Offer only one idea at a time.

✓ "Go big with your ideas." Fun and creative ideas are welcome.

✓ "Give attention" so another can make an offer and while they are making an offer.

✓ "Take attention" from the others so they may make an offer.

✓ Say, "Yes, and..."

✓ Build off the preceding offer and not try to plan ahead.

✓ Keep it about the "party." Stay focused on what they are planning and not go off on a tangent.

ADAPTATIONS & INTEGRATIONS

RELATED CONTENT REVIEW

Integrating the concepts and structures of improv with curricular content will enable students to more easily and efficiently transfer the skills developed during the games to use in other classroom activities and studies. This will also help transform the individual, and also the culture of the class, as students continue to develop the skills discussed in *Chapters 3* and *4*.

Using "Yes, and..." to format a review helps establish preexisting knowledge or proficiency among the students and review content from previous sessions. Teachers can often predict which students will be raising their hands during a review. "Yes, and..." encourages the participation of all, thus giving the teacher the information they seek while keeping the students engaged. Integrating the Yes, and-Planning structure can be done at the beginning of class as a review or throughout class as material is covered. Have students say "Yes, and..." before each offer until it seems that they have internalized it. Some students will continue saying it, even when they do not need to. At least you know what they are thinking.

This review structure is also very useful during oral reading assignments. After one or more readers have read, ask the class for an offer of just one piece of information that was just read, and start building the review from there. It's a great way for students who are auditory learners and/or struggling readers to stay engaged and eventually become more eager to read.

EXAMPLES

English/Language Arts: Romeo and Juliet

Teacher: What did we just read? What is one thing you remember or found interesting?
Student A: Juliet is on her balcony.
Student D: Yes, and she's a Capulet
Student E: Yes, and Romeo is a Montague.
Student M: Soliloquy
Student L: "What's in a name?"
Student C: Yes, and they realize that they are in love with each other.

Math/Geometry: Triangles

Teacher: Today we learned about triangles. What is one thing you remember?
Student A: Triangle
Student D: Yes, and triangles have three sides.
Student E: Yes, and right triangle.
Student M: Yes, and acute angle.

Student A: Yes, and obtuse angle.

Student L: Yes, and equilateral triangle.

Student G: Yes, and a right triangle has 90 degrees.

Social Studies/History: World History

Teacher: Yesterday, we discussed Egypt. What is one thing you remember about Egypt?

Student A: Egypt is on the Mediterranean Sea.

Student D: Yes, and the Nile River is in Egypt.

Student E: Yes, and the river dumps silt.

Student M: There is a delta at the end of the river.

Student A: The Nile supplies water for crops.

Student L: There is a desert in Egypt.

SEQUENTIAL CONTENT REVIEW

Students use the structure of Yes, And-Planning to create a sequential recall of content. For example, the students work in collaboration (pairs, small groups, entire class) and recall the sequence of a historical event, a work of literature, a scientific principle, a mathematical concept, etc. Students could say, "Yes and..." before each offer if they choose.

EXAMPLES

Science: The Water Cycle

Student A: The sun comes out and evaporates the water on the ground.

Student B: Yes, and the evaporated water travels up through the air.

Student C: Yes, and the air is cooler the higher it goes, causing the evaporated water to condense into water droplets.

Student D: Yes, and every water droplet forms around a dust particle.

Student B: The water droplets gather together and form clouds.

Student E: Yes, and when the cloud darkens at the bottom it means the cloud is heavy with water droplets.

Student F: Yes, and it begins to rain.

BRAINSTORMING

Brainstorming often follows a random structure supported by Zip-Zap-Zop *(p. 116),* whereby ideas will be random, unrelated, and individual. A brainstorming session that incorporates "Yes, and..."is a collaborative effort with the group building upon the ideas offered before them. Both are effective in different ways and are not exclusive. A random session helps get a lot of individual ideas presented, then a "Yes, and..." structured session could see the further collaborative integration and expansion of those ideas.

WE ARE...

We Are is a two-person storytelling game in which students create a story by each offering only one word at a time during alternating turns. In We Are, students are introduced to basic story structure. Responsible for adding only one word at a time, students are compelled to listen to each other's "offer." Speaking only one word at a time breaks students of the belief that they must create or control the entire story; sometimes, it is the verbally proficient students who are challenged by this game because they often prefer to create longer lines of thought. Students with lower verbal skills gain confidence, as they are only responsible for one word, and their offers must be accepted and not disregarded by the other students.

* The rule of "Yes, and..." transitions from being an external prompt to an internal prompt.

* Students are introduce to basic story elements (CROW) and the three-step story structure that will be used in games #2–#5.

* Students who are not fluent in English may find one-word games difficult, and other students in their group may be frustrated with their offers if their offers contain mistakes in syntax, tense, etc. English language learners find more success in the story games, where their offers will be longer phrases and sentences, as in games #4 and #5. In those games others will be better able to understand the meaning of their offer and add to it.

GAME EXAMPLE

Two student stand next to each other in front of room and face the audience and the teacher. They should stand as close to each other as they are comfortable. Although this game could be played while seated, when the students are in a standing position they can more easily add movement in order to act out their offers as they tell the story. Some students will have an easier time telling the story if they are permitted to act it out or add physical gestures. Physical contact is not required, but the two participants could hook inside arms while they stand facing the audience. Hooking arms reminds them they are creating and acting the story together, as well keeping any movement somewhat contained and limited. If the students are allowed to act out their story, they do so while remaining in place.

Student A	Student B	Action
We...	are...	*Students stand facing the class.*
swimming...	in...	*Students begin swimming in place while still facing the audience.*
the...	ocean	
when...	suddenly,...	
a...	giant...	
octopus...	attacks.	*Students stop swimming and show an octopus attacking them.*
We...	tie...	
his...	tentacles...	*Students show themselves tying his tentacles.*
together...	and...	
we...	swim...	*Student show themselves swimming away, still in place.*
away.	The...	
End.		

NEW TERMS & TOPIC

CROW

CROW is an acronym for **Character, Relationship, Objective, and Where.** CROW must be established within the first few lines of dialogue during the story games.

- ✓ **C** What kind of characters are present?

- ✓ **R** What kinds of relationships are present?

- ✓ **O** What is the objective of the characters?

- ✓ **W** Where is the location of the story?

In the following example both students work together and create CROW in two lines of dialogue. A general rule is to establish CROW in the first three lines of dialogue. When CROW fails to be established the story wanders aimlessly, becoming confusing and frustrating for the students as they struggle to have it make sense.

Student A: Hey sis, hold this ladder while I try to rescue Fluffy.	Characters: sister/sister or sister/brother Relationship: siblings Objective: to climb
Student B: I wish mom's cat wouldn't climb up on our roof to chase birds.	Where: their home's roof

THREE-STEP STORY STRUCTURE

1. Establish CROW (character, relationship, objective and where).
2. Create a problem.
3. Solve it.

ENDING A SENTENCE

The student should indicate the end of a sentence with their vocal intonation. Students need to stress the last word of a sentence. If they don't, they will create a rather long run-on thought that will become confusing to all students involved in creating and listening to the story.

MOVING A SCENE FORWARD WITH ACTION

"Move the scene forward" is a common direction given to the students composing a story. The use of action, specifically action verbs, helps the plot of a story develop rapidly and keep moving until a resolution has been created. When students avoid the use of action, their stories become wordy, muddled, and stagnant. Students learn the use and power of action verbs rather quickly during We Are and Volley Word. When stories are moved forward with the use of action, students may be able to tell a complete story in three sentences. An example of moving a scene forward with action might sound like this.

Examples taken from Volley Word

Without Action: The... tiger... was... coming... at... us... and... he... wanted... to... attack... us... so... he... started... to... attack.

With action: The... tiger... attacked... us.

It is important for the students to thoroughly understand this concept. When they offer phrases and sentences in the more advanced story games, they will be tempted to return to a passive voice.

Student A: The detective found footprints.	Action
Student B: He followed them.	Action

An example of **not** *moving a scene forward with action* might sound like this:

Student A:	The detective found footprints.	Action
Student B:	So he thought maybe he should follow them.	No action
Student C:	So he decided that he should follow them.	No action
Student D:	He followed them.	Action

Student B and C did not move the story forward. Their offers did not contribute any action or new information.

STUDENT NOTEBOOKS

As students start to play the more complex storytelling and scene-based games they will need to consistently apply story elements. If the games are being integrated into a classroom or supplemental program, and especially if the focus is on writing skills, then it would be helpful for students to keep a notebook or a section of a notebook dedicated to the story elements. Below are suggestions on how to organize a notebook section. If notebooks are unavailable, reproducible worksheets are provided in *Part 3*.

Section 1: CROW

Dedicate a separate page for each of the following elements of CROW: Characters, Relationships, Objectives, Where. Students should try to list as many as they can individually or in collaboration with others. Allowing at least a full page to each element of CROW will allow the list to be expanded.

Examples of Characters:

Astronaut	Dancer
Explorer	Vampire
Dentist	Pirate
Painter	Doctor
Tennis Player	Elf
Super Hero	Cheerleader
Clown	Politician
Secret Agent	Farmer

Examples of Relationships:

Romantic	Siblings
Coach/Player	Rivals
Best Friends	Arch Enemies
Parent/Child	Husband/Wife
Waitress/Customer	Teacher/Student
Doctor/Patient	Teammates

Examples of Objectives:

To bake a cake	To pass a test
To win a game	To find true love
To slay a dragon	To find the treasure
To solve a mystery	To save the world
To break a spell	To escape

Examples of Where:

Jungle	Beach
Classroom	Movie Theater
Cafeteria	Castle
Haunted Mansion	Laundromat
Football game	Doctor's Office
Miniature Golf Course	Submarine

Section 2: Things found in Where

After students create a list of general "where" they should begin to think of things that can be found in those "where." Below are a few examples.

Jungle: vines, caves, wild animals, quicksand, lost civilizations, ancient treasure, archaeologist, scientist, poisonous plants, snakes, insects...

Beach: sand, ocean, seashells, lifeguard chairs, lifeguards, badge checkers, suntan lotion, beach blankets, beach umbrellas, beach chairs, volleyball nets, bonfires...

Classroom: blackboard, chalk, pointer, maps, globes, desks with gum stuck to the bottom, books, pencils, pens, crayons, bulletin boards, teacher's desk, closet...

GAME PLAN

FOCUS:	
1. "Yes, and..." (as an internal prompt)	**GOALS/OBJECTIVES:** See Rubric
2. Establishing CROW	
3. Three-Step Story Structure	**STUDENT POSITIONING:**
4. Moving a scene/story forward by using action	Minimal space in front of class

DIRECTIONS:

Create Relevance

If you don't know CROW, you don't know what is going on.

Relevance can be created by helping students realize that they already react to stories or situations where they are uncertain of CROW. For example, show students a middle portion of a movie; give them a midsection of a story to read; ask them to observe people they do not know well interacting; or use the guided question format outlined below. Any of these methods exemplify the importance of establishing CROW of a situation or story in order to get or keep someone's attention.

> » Raise your hand if you have ever written or read a story that didn't make much sense; you may have gotten lost when reading it, or it just rambled on.

> » If you were watching TV and you were changing the channels and you came across a movie but it had started 40 minutes before, would you watch it or keep looking for something else to watch? Why wouldn't you know what was going on? What wouldn't you know?

> » Students start giving answers and the teacher starts to relate their answers to story elements and to story structure. Teachers also construct a sample story using CROW and the three-step story structure as an example for the students before playing the game. See steps 7–9.

> > Story Elements: CROW (Character, Relationship, Objective, Where)
> > Story Structure:
> >
> > **1.** Establish CROW
> >
> > **2.** Create a Problem
> >
> > **3.** Solve It

Introduce Game

1. *Demonstrate:* Follow steps 2–11.

2. The teacher models telling and writing a story on the board so students can see the simple three-step structure.

3. Two students volunteer and stand side by side facing the class. Follow steps 2–10.

4. *Audience Offer:* The class offers "where" they want the two students to be.

5. Each student may only speak one alternating word at a time. They may also act out the story together.

6. The game begins when one student says, "We..." and the other student responds, "... are..." They then must quickly establish **CROW.**

7. A strong suggestion for format is, "We are... **(OBJECTIVE)**. An action verb should be used for the Objective. Example*: "We... are... swimming....* Then add the **(WHERE)** the class had offered. *"We... are... swimming... in... the... ocean..."*

8. After *Crow* is established, they need to complete the three-step story structure. They now need to create a **problem.** For example: *"We... are... swimming...in... the... ocean.* ***Suddenly,****... a... giant... shark... attacks.*

9. After that, they must now work together to **resolve the problem.** It might sound like, *"We... are... swimming... in... the... ocean... when... suddenly,... a...giant... shark... attacks. We... hug... the... shark. It... begins... to... cry. We... swim... away.*

10. Optional: Have students then add a **moral** to the story. For example, "Even... sharks... like... hugs." This is a very simple example, but the students' versions should not be much, if any longer.

11. *End with Acknowledgment:* The teacher can indicate the end of the game with a simple, "Give them a hand!" Audience and storytellers applaud one another.

Practice

12. After students have demonstrated the game, continue until all students have had a turn. Repeat steps 2–13.

13. *Feedback:* Discuss whether the items in the "Focus" section of the Game Plan were achieved. "Was CROW established?" "Was the story structure followed?" The rubric can provide additional detail to the discussion and/or serve as a self, group, or teacher assessment.

COACHING & NOTES

COACHING:

Example: with optional in place movement

Student A	Student B	Teacher	Action
We...	are...		
flying...	through space...	**One Word. "We are flying..."**	
	through...		*Pretends to fly*
space...	in...		
a...	jungle.	**Show us flying through a jungle**	*Shows flying through trees and vines*
		Create a problem	
Suddenly,...	a...		
dinosaur grabs us...		**One Word. "Suddenly, a..."**	
dinosaur...	eats...		
us.			*Stops flying and shows being eaten by a dinosaur*
		Solve the problem.	
	We...		
tickle...	his...		
tummy...	and...	**Show us**	*Tickling tummy*
he...	throws...		
us...	up.		*Being thrown up*
The...	End.		

TEACHER'S NOTES:

Coach students to:

   ✓ Establish CROW, create a problem, and solve it.

   ✓ Offer only one word at a time.

   ✓ "Yes, and...". Do not allow denials. They must listen to and build off their partner's offer and not try to plan the direction of the story by themselves.

   ✓ If this game seems complicated at first because of the optional but recommended movement, then remove the movement. Have the students tell the story and introduce the movement after a few run-throughs.

#3

VOLLEY WORD & *improv writing*

Volley Word is a two-person storytelling game in which students create a story by each offering only one word at a time during alternating turns. A **Collaborative Writing Activity** helps students transfer storytelling and fluency skills expressed orally to writing. Speaking only one word at a time breaks students of the belief that they must create or control the entire story themselves or that they must plan out the entire story in their head before beginning to write.

* CROW and the three-step story structure is reinforced orally and in writing. Students also practice identifying CROW and story strucure through listening and reading.

* Students continue to practice "Yes, and..." as an internal prompt by adding only one word at a time.

* The one-word games of *We Are* and *Volley Word* are integral for building respect, tolerance, and an overall cohesiveness within the class.

* Students who are not fluent in English will find one-word games difficult, and other students in their group will be frustrated with their offers if their offers contain mistakes in syntax, tense, etc. English language learners find more success in the story games where their offers will be longer phrases and sentences that allow others to understand the meaning of their offer and add to it, as in games #4 and #5.

GAME EXAMPLE

This game is played with two students either standing or sitting side by side in front of the class. Standing is recommended because it give students who are more kinesthetic the opportunity to make subtle movements or gestures while creating the story.

Student A	Student B
Sam...	the...
sloth...	slept...
on...	an...
old...	rocket.
Suddenly,...	the...

rocket...	blasted...
off.	Sam...
clung...	to...
the...	rocket.
He...	shimmied...
to...	the...
nose...	and...
swung...	the...
nose...	toward...
home.	He...
landed...	safely.
The...	End.

NEW TERMS & TOPICS

DENIAL

1: Saying "No..." or "Yes, but..."
2: Negating the offer
3: Fighting
4: Killing off main characters:

Like We Are, Volley Word is a one-word story game and because of that, denials 1, 2 and 3 should not be an issue. Killing off the main character, however, is a form of denial that is possible with this game. Simply remind them it's a denial and not to kill off the main character.

STUDENT NOTEBOOKS

Section 3: Collaborative and Individual Written Stories

Students should dedicate a section of their notebook to their collaborative and individual stories. Using a notebook section to collect the students' stories offers the following advantages over the use of individual sheets of paper, which are more likely to be lost or destroyed.

✓ Notebooks are easier and neater to pass from student to student when doing the collaborative writing activities.

✓ Students and teachers will be able to view progress from page to page.

GAME PLAN

FOCUS:	GOALS/OBJECTIVES: See Rubric
1. "Yes, and…"	
2. Establishing CROW	STUDENT POSITIONING:
3. Three-Step Story Structure	Minimal space in front of class
4. Move Forward with Action	At desks seated or standing

DIRECTIONS:

Introduce Game

1. *Demonstrate:* Follow steps 2–9.

2. The teacher models telling and writing a story on the board so students can see its structure.

3. One pair of students volunteer or are chosen. The students face their partner.

4. *Audience Offer:* The class is asked to suggest "an unusual animal."

5. Using only one word at a time and taking alternating turns, the pair begins to tell a story about the animal.

6. Students must work to establish CROW, move the story forward through action, create a conflict, and resolve the conflict.

7. The students conclude the story on their own, but are guided by the teacher to follow the three-step story structure introduced in We Are. Stories are usually around five or six lines in this game.

8. *End with Acknowledgment:* The teacher can indicate the end of the game with a simple, "Give them a hand!" Allow the audience to applaud and also the storytellers to applaud the audience for their suggestion. The teacher and all students positively acknowledge one anothers' efforts.

Practice

9. Repeat steps 2–11 until all students have participated.

10. *Feedback:* Discuss if topics of "Focus" were achieved. "Was there a problem?" "Did they solve it?" The rubric can provide additional detail to the discussion and/or serve as a self, group, or teacher assessment.

Apply

11. *Transference:* Students transition oral skills to writing with the Volley Word Writing Activity. Directions can be found under "Adaptations and Integrations."

COACHING & NOTES

COACHING:

Student A	Student B	Teacher
Sam...	the...	
sloth...	slept in a ...	**One word**
	slept...	
on...	an...	
old...	rocket.	
		Create a problem
Suddenly,...	the...	
rocket...	blasted...	
off.	Sam...	
died.		**Denial. Don't kill main character**
clung...	to...	
the...	rocket.	**Solve the problem**
He...	shimmied...	
to...	the...	
nose...	and...	
he...	felt...	
scared...	and...	
he...	felt..	**Move forward with action**
strong.	He...	
swung...	the...	
nose...	toward...	
home.		**End it.**
	He...	
landed...	safely.	
The...	End.	

TEACHER'S NOTES:

Coach students to:

✓ Establish CROW, create a problem, and solve it.

✓ Offer only one word at a time.

✓ Build off their partner's offer and not try to plan the direction of the story by themselves.

ADAPTATIONS & INTEGRATIONS

Adapting the games into writing activities will help students transfer developed skills to their writing.

IMPROV STORY WRITING:

FOCUS: 1. "Yes, and…" 2. Establishing CROW 3. Story Structure	**GOALS/OBJECTIVES:** See Rubric **MATERIALS:** Notebooks and pen/pencil **STUDENT POSITIONING:** At desks seated with group

DIRECTIONS

Collaborative Writing Activity

1. Students form groups of two and an odd group of three if necessary.

2. On the top of their paper, each student writes their name and the names of the other students in their group.

3. The class offers an animal.

4. Each student titles their paper with the name of the game and the type of animal chosen by the class. This allows questions about spelling the name of the animal to be addressed.

5. *Reading/Writing Fluency:* Set a passing pattern. On the teacher's command, each student writes the first word of the story and passes the paper to the next student. The students read what has been written and adds a word to each story before passing it along, at their own pace. This works quite smoothly if the students share similar reading and writing levels. Although students are only writing one word at a time, they are still responsible for contributing an element of CROW, as well as creating a conflict and finding a resolution.This continues until the teacher tells the students to begin to work toward ending the story.

6. *End with Acknowledgment:* When the groups have finished ending their stories, students thank their group members and retrieve the story they started.

7. *Scanning Skills:* Have students box all words or phrases that create CROW, and underline all words and phrases that form steps 2 and 3 of the three-step story structure. Students should be able to tell what the main idea of the story is when these terms are read aloud.

8. *Feedback:* Students and teacher discuss if topics of "Focus" were achieved. "Was CROW established?" "Was "Yes, and…," used throughout the story?" The rubric can provide additional detail to the discussion and/or serve as a self, group, or teacher assessment.

DID YOU HEAR THE ONE ABOUT...?
& *improv writing*

Did You Hear the One About...? is a storytelling game in which approximately four to seven students stand in single file, one behind the other. Students create a story by offering phrases and sentences during their turn. **Collaborative and Individual Story-Writing Activities** help students translate storytelling and fluency skills expressed orally into writing.

⁎ The students' responsibility for including essential story elements (CROW) increases along with the complexity of the stories' structure in both the oral and writing games.

⁎ Listening and reading skills are further practiced and developed as students begin to offer phrases and sentences orally and in writing.

⁎ Game structure can be used for integration with curricular content.

⁎ Story genres/styles may be incorporated after they are introduced and practiced in game #5 Story-Story *(p. 103)*.

GAME EXAMPLE

Four or more students stand in a line. The first student faces the audience and the other three or more line up behind the first. The teacher asks for an audience offer of a boring object or a boring gift they wouldn't want to receive.

Did You Hear the One About... the Sock?

Student A: Sam the Sock sat in the sock drawer. He wanted to play.

Student B: Suddenly, he realized his pair was gone.

Student C: He looked everywhere in the sock drawer for him, but couldn't find him.

Student D: So he jumped out of the drawer to the floor and slid under the bed.

Student E: Then suddenly, he was grabbed and put on a smelly foot.

Student F: It was his boy and he was going out to play. Sam was confused because he had no pair, but when he looked over to the other foot he saw...

Student G: ...Sally the Sock. Sam blushed. He always had a crush on Sally. Sally...

Student H: ... told Sam that his pair was now a sock puppet for a school project.

Teacher: End it.

Student I: But Sam didn't care because now he could go out and play with Sally. Sam and Sally played happily ever after. The End.

Did You Hear the One About the... Toothbrush?

Genre: Mystery

Stories can be told in a specific style or genre *(pp. 103-105)*, but only after students have practiced this game and Story-Story. After students have practiced adding genre in Story-Story they should return to this game to add a genre or style.

Student A: It was a dark and stormy night. Teresa the Toothbrush sat on the cold sink in the dark. Suddenly, she heard a scream.

Student B: She looked around and saw Miguel the Mouthwash was leaking all over the floor. He had been broken.

Student C: Teresa saw blue footprints leading to the bathroom door.

Student D: She followed them and then went to the phone to call the police, but the phone was dead.

Student E: She returned to the bathroom and saw something had been written on the mirror. It...

Student F: ...was a smiley face.

Student G: Teresa thought, "How mean."

Student H: She was mad and wanted to find out who broke Miguel, so she decided to investigate herself.

Student I: She heard a noise coming from the...

Student J: ...shower. She approached and pulled the curtain back.

Teacher: End it.

Student K: There was Fred the Floss soaked in blue mouthwash. He did it. He was jealous that Miguel the mouthwash was stronger and mintier than he was. The End.

NEW TERMS & TOPICS

DENIAL

Students in this game offer phrases and sentences. Denials are therefore more frequent and might often take the form of numbers 1, 2, 3, and 4.

1: Saying "No..." or "Yes, but..."
Student A: Purple Beard was the meanest pirate to sail the seas.
Student B: No, he wasn't.

Student A: Purple Beard was the meanest pirate to sail the seas.
Student B: Yeah, but Orange Beard was meaner.

2: Negating the offer
Student A: The professor went into the lab and...
Student B: then he went skiing in the Alps.

Student A: The gnome disappeared, never to be seen again.
Student B: But then the gnome came back.

3: Fighting
Student A: Suddenly, the phone rang.
Student B: No, it didn't.
Student A: Yes, it did.

4: Killing off main characters
Student A: Once upon a time, a princess rode on her unicorn through the enchanted forest...
Student B: She found a poison apple, ate it and died. A powerful wizard ruled the land.

GENRE/STORY STYLE

When students are comfortable with the structure of this game and have already learned and participated in Story-Story, they may choose to add a genre *(pp. 103-105)*. The audience chooses the object, but allows the first storyteller to set the genre. This serves as a nice surprise for the audience, as well as the rest of the players. For example, if the object given was a paperclip and the student chose the genre of "science fiction," the story may begin like this...

"In a galaxy far, far away, a paperclip spiraled through space searching for..."

STUDENT NOTEBOOKS

Section 4: Journals: Keeping a daily journal provides an opportunity for students to practice transferring the fluency skills developed through this sequence of games to other writing assignments.

GAME PLAN

FOCUS:	
1. "Yes, and..." 2. Establishing CROW. 3. Three-Step Story Structure 4. Moving Story Forward with Action 5. Add Genre (optional)	**GOALS/OBJECTIVES:** See Rubric **STUDENT POSITIONING:** Open space in front of class

DIRECTIONS:

Introduce Game

1. *Demonstrate:* Follow steps 2–9.

2. Approximately four to eight students stand in a straight line, one behind the other, with the first student facing the class. This can also be set up with the students facing one another in a circle if there are not enough students to make up an audience.

3. *Audience Offer:* Ask the students who are not participating (the audience) to suggest a "boring object" or a "gift they did not want."

4. The teacher says, "Did you hear the one about... *the paperclip*?"

5. The first student starts the story, establishing as much CROW as possible. The student continues to tell the story until the teacher signals to that student that their turn has ended by pointing to the back of the line.

6. The next student continues the story exactly where the other student left off and establishes any remaining CROW.

7. Step 5 is repeated until all students have gone at least once.

8. Students follow story structure by introducing a conflict(s) and working toward a resolution. The teacher chooses when to end the story by saying to the next speaking student, "End It."

9. *End with Acknowledgment:* The teacher can indicate the completion of the game with a simple, "Give them a hand!" Allow the audience to applaud, and also the storytellers to applaud the audience for their suggestion. The teacher and all students positively acknowledge each other's efforts.

Practice

10. Repeat steps 2–11 until all students have played.

11. *Feedback:* Students and teacher discuss if topics of "Focus" were achieved. "Was CROW established?" "Was "Yes, and...," used throughout the story?" The rubric can provide additional detail to the discussion and/or serve as a self, group, or teacher assessment.

Apply

12. *Transference:* To transfer skills developed through the game, facilitate the following activities presented in "Adaptations and Integrations."

COACHING & NOTES

COACHING:

Genre: Mystery

Student A: It was a dark and stormy night. Teresa the Toothbrush sat on the cold sink in the dark. Suddenly, she heard a scream.

Student B: No, it was more like an explosion.

Teacher: Denial. "She heard a scream"

Student G: She looked around and saw Miguel the Mouthwash was leaking all over the floor. He had been broken.

Student C: Teresa saw blue footprints leading to the bathroom door.

Student D: She followed them and then...

Student F: ..went to the phone to call the police, but the phone was dead.

Student E: She returned to the bathroom and saw something had been written on the mirror. It...

Student B: ...was a smiley face.

Student D: Teresa called the cops.

Teacher: Denial. The phone is already dead. "It was a smiley face."

Student G: Teresa thought, "How mean."

Student H: She was mad and wanted to find out who broke Miguel, so she decided to investigate herself.

Student I: She heard a noise coming from the...

Student D: ...spaceship.

Teacher: Denial...negating of story style.

Student A: shower. She approached and pulled the curtain back.

Teacher: End it.

Student G: There was Fred the Floss soaked in blue mouthwash. He did it. He was jealous that Miguel the mouthwash was stronger and mintier than him. The End.

TEACHER'S NOTES

✓ It is less confusing if the story is told in the third person.

✓ Students should establish CROW by the first two or three storytellers.

✓ Remind the students that too many characters may get confusing

✓ Students must be familiar with the chosen genre.

✓ Remind students to not "kill off" the main character.

✓ Reinforce the importance of listening and using "Yes and..."

✓ Suggest they move the story line forward by using action.

✓ Act it!

> When it is a student's turn, allow them the option to act out the story as they tell it by adding movement. For example, if the story was about a "lightbulb," and the student began, "Lenny the Lightbulb turned and turned into the socket...," the student while he was speaking could become Lenny the Lightbulb and turn around as if he was being turned into the socket. Some students will have an easier time telling the story if they are permitted to act it out kinesthetically in place.

ADAPTATIONS & INTEGRATIONS

Adapting the games into writing activities and integrating content into the game structures will help students transfer developed skills to their writing. Types of integrations and adaptations offered include:

✓ Collaborative story writing

✓ Individual story writing

✓ Content Integration: Ideas contained in Story-Story *(p. 102)*.

IMPROV STORY WRITING

FOCUS:	**GOALS/OBJECTIVES:** See Rubric
1. "Yes, and..."	
2. Establishing CROW.	**MATERIALS:** Notebooks & pen/pencil
3. Three-Step Story Structure	
4. Moving Story Forward with Action	**STUDENT POSITIONING:** Seated at desks in groups of three to five
5. Add Genre (optional)	

DIRECTIONS:

Collaborative Writing Activity

1. Students form groups of three to five.

2. The class chooses an object.

3. Each student writes on the top of their paper the names of the other students in their group.

4. Each student titles his/her paper, Did You Hear the One About the (Chosen Object)?

5. *Reading/Writing Fluency:* The teacher tells them to begin writing the story.

6. After an appropriate period of time, the teacher asks them to "pause." The teacher then tells them, "Wherever you are is fine. Please pass your paper." This lessens the "But I'm not done!" feeling the students may express the first few times doing an activity like this. The teacher then asks the students to thank the person who passed a story to them. ** Students may write at different speeds, so some may contribute a few sentences, while others might only be able to write a few words. **

7. When a student receives a new story, that student now reads from the beginning of the story and continues the story, adding any missing elements of CROW and moving the story forward following the three-step structure and using action.

8. Steps 6 and 7 are repeated continuously every few minutes for a total of about 10 minutes, until the teacher tells the students to, "End the story." Each student then writes an ending to the story in front of them.

9. *End with Acknowledgment:* When the groups have finished ending their stories, students thank their group members and retrieve the story they started.

10. Give students the opportunity to read aloud the story they began or ended.

11. *Scanning Skills:* Have students box all words or phrases that create CROW, and underline all words and phrases that form steps 2 and 3 of the three-step story structure. Students should be able to tell what the main idea of the story is when these terms are read aloud.

12. *Feedback:* Students and teacher discuss if topics of "Focus" were achieved. The rubric can provide additional detail to the discussion and/or serve as a self, group, or teacher assessment.

13. *Acknowledgment:* The teacher can indicate the end of the activity with a simple, "Give yourselves a hand!" The teacher and all students positively acknowledge one anothers' efforts.

DIRECTIONS:

Individual Story-Writing Activity

1. The class or each student chooses a boring object.

2. Each student titles their paper, Did You Hear the One about the (Chosen Object)?

3. Have students then write their own story about the object. Whether they are writing in class or at home, give them a time limit similar to what they had in class in which to write and finish the story; for example 10 minutes.

4. *Scanning Skills:* When students are done, they will pass their story to another student. The other student checks for CROW, conflict, resolution, and genre (if applicable).

5. *Rewriting:* Each student rewrites their story with any necessary corrections (optional).

STORY-STORY & *improv writing*

The *Story-Story* games are genre-based, storytelling games that involve a larger number of students. Students create a story by offering phrases and sentences during their turns. **Collaborative and Individual Writing Activities** help students transfer storytelling and fluency skills expressed orally to writing.

* Story styles/genres are introduced and applied.

* *Story-Story* further expands the students' responsibility for including essential story elements and increases the complexity of the stories' structure; thus developing greater narrative skills through listening, speaking, reading, and writing.

* Game structure can be used for integration with curricular content.

* Students practice the transfer of developed skills to individual writing.

GAME EXAMPLE

GENRE: FAIRY TALE

Student A:	Once upon a time, Princess Gwen skipped through the enchanted forest, picking wild flowers, when suddenly,...
Student C:	...a tree grabbed her. She struggled but it wouldn't let go.
Student F:	Then a witch appeared. The witch was jealous of her beauty and turned Princess Gwen into a...
Student J:	...rock.
Student D:	Suddenly, a giant, fire-breathing dragon swooped down and...
Student E:	...scared the witch away.
Student F:	The dragon grabbed the rock and brought it back to its lair.
Student A:	The dragon was actually a prince under the witch's spell.
Teacher:	End it.
Student B:	The princess' fairy godmother appeared and released both the prince and princess from the spell. They lived happily ever after. The End.

GENRE: SCIENCE FICTION

Student A: Captain Quasar, commander of the starfleet, was patrolling the Quadrant X when...

Student D: a distress call came from Mars.

Student E: It was his wife. She wanted him to pick up dinner.

Student A: So he stopped at McMars and got dinner, but when he got home...

Student B: ...he realized his family had been brainwashed and were now controlled by an alien species.

Student E: He ran back to his ship and looked for an antidote to the alien brain...

Student C: ...washing. He loaded the antidote into his beam gun.

Student A: Captain Quasar beamed himself into this living room and pointed his beam gun at the reflective panels of a satellite that would then shower his home with the antidote particles to free his family.

Teacher: End it.

Student D: The radiation from the particles freed his family and they all went out for pizza. The End.

NEW TERMS & TOPICS

GENRES /STORY STYLES

This game requires the use of a story style or genre. Once students understand how to use style when telling and writing a story, they can add it to *Did You Hear the One About*. When students create a story in a certain style or genre, they build a greater awareness of the particular elements and details of CROW and the commonalities of story lines within a given genre. Choose genres for fun or to reflect the curricular goals of the class. Fairy tale is a genre style that is familiar to most students in all grade levels. Even if fairy tales are not part of the curriculum, this genre is a good one to start with, even for high school age students. Other genre/storystyles might include: mystery, romance, action-adventure, science fiction, etc. To increase difficulty and curricular relevance, story could be

told in the style of studied playwrights or authors: Stephen King, Shakespeare, Tennessee Williams, etc.

DENIAL

Students in this game offer phrases and sentences. Denials are therefore more frequent and might often take the form of numbers 1, 2, 3, and 4. Examples are given in Game 4 *(pp. 96-97)*.

1. Saying "No..." or "Yes, but..."

2. Negating the offer

3. Fighting

4. Killing off the main characters

STUDENT NOTEBOOKS

Section 4: Genres/Story Style

Before adding a genre to a game, students should collaboratively or individually make lists of the following information for genres/story styles they might use in a game.

          C: What kinds of characters are present?
          R: What kinds of relationships are present?
          O: What is the objective of the characters?
          W: Where is the location of the story?
          What kind of things would be there?
          What are common names for the characters?

* Avoid using names of classmates.

* Avoid using names of famous characters like Cinderella, Snow White, Frankenstein, Harry Potter, etc. Sometimes students feel obliged to retell the famous stories they are taken from instead of creating their own.

Fairy Tale:

Characters: Princess, king, dragon, knight, witches, fairies, giant, fairy godmother, troll...
Relationships: Romantic, enemies, rivals, friends, parent and child, stepmother and child...
Objectives: To rescue the princess, to slay the dragon, to no longer be poor, to be king...
Where: In a castle, in the woods, in a cave, in an enchanted forest, in a dungeon...
Things: Magic spells, potions, swords, magic beans, unicorns, gold, genie lamps...
Names: Princess...., Sir..., etc. ...

Science Fiction:

Characters: Mad scientist, monsters, aliens, zombies, space commanders, giant insects...
Relationships: Romantic, enemies, creator & monster, old rivals, friends...

Objectives: To rule the world, to seek revenge, to survive, to shrink people...
Where(s): In a castle, in space, in a basement, in the woods, at the bottom of the ocean...
Things: Giant electrical switches, potions, worm-holes, space ships, radiation...
Names: Doctor, Commander..., etc. ...

Mystery:

Characters: Detective, butler, maid, guests, police, private detectives, ghosts...
Relationships: Romantic, enemies, rivals, best friends...
Objectives: To solve a crime, to solve the mystery, to right a wrong, to find the truth...
Where(s): In a mansion, in a tree/club house, in a library, in a secret passage way...
Things: Phones that are dead, secret rooms, footprints, phone records...
Names: Inspector..., Madam ..., Officer ..., etc. ...

Action/Adventure:

Characters: Secret agents, archaeologists, treasure hunters...
Relationships: Romantic, enemies, rivals, friends...
Objectives: To find the treasure, to prevent war or the world's total destruction...
Where(s): In a jungle, in an ancient tomb, on a wealthy estate...
Things: Fast cars, gadgets that are weapons, rolling boulders, pits of snakes,...
Names: Professor..., Warrior Princess..., Agent..., etc. ...

GAME PLAN

FOCUS: 1. "Yes, and..." 2. Establish CROW 3. Story Structure 4. Moving story with action 5. Genre/Story Style	**GOALS/OBJECTIVES:** See Rubric **STUDENT POSITIONING:** Story-Story: open space in front of class Story-Circle: seated at desks Story- "Yerr... Out": open space in front of class

DIRECTIONS:

Creating Relevance

Stories have style, too.

Students are very familiar with fashion styles. A style has specific elements, as well as a distinct structure. Style can tell us about a person before we even speak to them. Stories have style, too, and students are already familiar with the elements of genre/story styles through a variety of media. Guided questioning or an activity that makes students aware of their existing knowledge about style in general and about specific story styles/genres will help prepare them for this game.

> » Teacher: What kind of stories, movies, books, video games do you like?

> » Students: Horror, Romance, Fantasy….

> » Teacher: Why do you like Fantasy? What makes a fantasy story a fantasy story?

> » Students: magic, action, good triumphs over evil, creatures…

> » Teacher: (Discuss elements of CROW for a specific genre. Make lists on board. Have students make lists in their notebooks).

Introduce Game

1. *Demonstrate:* Follow steps 2–8.

2. Approximately five to seven volunteers model the game in front of class. They stand in a line with all students facing the class.

3. *Audience Offer:* The class chooses what genre of story they would like to hear.

4. The teacher faces the student line.

5. The teacher points to one student, who then begins telling the story. That student continues to tell the story until the teacher stops pointing at them and begins to point at another student.

6. That next student continues the story exactly where the first student ended and continues to tell the story until the teacher points at another student.

7. The teacher continues "conducting" the creation of this story until they point to a student and says "End it." That student resolves any pending conflicts and ends the story.

8. *End with Acknowledgment:* The teacher can indicate the end of the game with a simple, "Give them a hand!" Allow the class to applaud the storytellers, and the storytellers to applaud the class for their suggestion. The teacher and all students positively acknowledge one anothers' efforts.

Practice

9. Repeat steps 1–10 until all students have had a chance to participate.

10. *Feedback:* Students and teacher discuss if topics of "Focus" were achieved. "Was the story moved forward with action?" "Was the story style supported?" The rubric can provide additional detail to the discussion and/or serve as a self, group, or teacher assessment.

Apply

11. *Transference:* To transfer skills developed through the game, facilitate the activities presented in "Adaptations and Integrations."

✳ ✳ ✳ ✳ ✳ ✳ ✳ ✳ ✳ ✳

STORY-STORY VARIATIONS

Story-Story Circle (Lowest Threat)

DIRECTIONS: *Introduce this game only if some students resisted participating in the previous version.* This version engages students who resist getting in front of the class. It is less threatening because there is no audience.

- Students can offer as much or as little story line as they wish. They are in control.

- If a student's turn to offer is determined by a clockwise or counter clockwise passing pattern, "Yes, and..." will tend to be ignored as students stop listening to offers and are instead thinking about what they are going to say on their turn. Ignoring "Yes, and..." will result in limited skill development (social-emotional, performance, and literacy).

- Using a random pass format, like used in Zip-Zap-Zop, will encourage students to "Yes, and..."

1. Follow the general concept of *Story-Story* but eliminate the role of the teacher as story director.

2. Have the students sit in a circle as a class or in small groups at their desks.

3. One student starts the story. When that student wishes to stop they simply stop talking and look to the next student.

4. The next student continues the story until they stop on their own and then looks at, directing their attention to the next student.

5. Continue until all students have contributed.

6. When all have contributed at least once, the teacher directs one student to end the story.

Story-Story "Yerrr... Out !" (Most challenging and competitive)

DIRECTIONS: *Use only for fun after students have shown mastery of Story-Story.*

1. Follow Story-Story directions steps 2–5.

2. If the new student does not start with a word that makes sense with the preceding word, pauses too long, or says, "uh...," the teacher signals the class to say, "Yerrr... out!"

3. Continue the game until only one student remains standing. The last student standing finishes the story.

4. When the story is finished allow players and class to applaud one another.

COACHING & NOTES

COACHING:

Genre: Fairy Tale

Student A: Once upon a time, Cinderella...

Teacher: **Create an original character.**

Student A: Once upon a time, Princess Gwen skipped through the enchanted forest, picking wild flowers, when suddenly,...

Student C: ...a tree grabbed her. She struggled but it wouldn't let go.

Student F: Then a witch name Kayla appeared.

Teacher: **Don't use classmates' names.**

Student F: Then a witch appeared. The witch was jealous of her beauty and turned Princess Gwen into a...

Student J: ...Gwen tried to...

Teacher: **"Yes, and..." ...turned Princess Gwen into a...**

Student J: ...rock.

Student D: Suddenly, a giant, fire-breathing dragon swooped down and...

Student E: ...scared the witch away.

Student F: The dragon grabbed the rock and brought it back to its lair, dropping it on its pile of gold.

Student A: The dragon was actually a prince under the witch's spell.

Teacher: **End it.**

Student B: The princess's fairy godmother appeared and released both the prince and princess from the spell. They lived happily ever after. The End.

TEACHER'S NOTES:

✓ Students must be familiar with the chosen genre.

✓ Stories should be told in the third person. It is much less confusing for the students and the audience.

✓ Students should establish CROW by the first two or three storytellers.

✓ Remind students to not "kill off" the main character.

✓ Reinforce the importance of listening and using "Yes and..."

✓ Suggest they move the story line forward by using action.

✓ Remind the students that introducing too many characters may get confusing.

✓ Act it!

When it is a student's turn, allow them the option to act out the story as they tell it by adding movement. For example, if the story was a fairy tale and the student says, "Herfairy godmother waved her magic wand and ...." As the student says those words, they might act as if they were the fairy godmother waving her wand. **Some students will have an easier time telling the story if they are permitted to kinesthetically act it out in place. Students only move when they are the speaker and not someone else.

✓ Increasing Difficulty

Difficulty is easily increased when:

- The teacher stops a student in the middle of a sentence by pointing to the next student to continue at that point.

- The teacher stops a student in the middle of a word by pointing to the next student to finish the word and continue the story from that point.

- The teacher increases the rate of speed at which they switch pointing from one student to another.

✓ Note on Gender Differences

During the improv games of *Story-Story* and *Did You Hear the One About,* the group of students creating the story will more likely be composed of both boys and girls. This is good, as it will expose them to telling types of stories they might not choose. During the collaborative writing activity where they might choose their own groups, all-girl and all-boy groups tend to form. That works. Since each group might be given the opportunity to choose their own genre, boys tend to choose action/adventure stories and girls often write romances. Once, while playing Did You Hear the One About... the Sock?, a high school age group of girls collaboratively wrote a "Romeo and Juliet"- style story involving the sock and a do-rag that met in a dresser drawer. Remind students to use classroom-appropriate language and topics, and also to not get caught up in violence and gore. They need to keep the story moving forward.

ADAPTATIONS & INTEGRATIONS

Adapting the games into writing activities and integrating content into the game structures will help students transfer developed skills to their writing. Types of integrations and adaptations offered include:

✓ Collaborative story writing

✓ Individual story writing

✓ Content integration: ideas for how curricular content can be integrated into the games

IMPROV STORY WRITING

FOCUS:	GOALS/OBJECTIVES: See Rubric
1. "Yes, and…"	
2. Establish CROW	MATERIALS: Notebooks and pen/pencil
3. Story Structure	
4. Moving story with action	STUDENT POSITIONING OPTIONS:
5. Genre/Story Style	At desks in groups of three to five

DIRECTIONS:

Collaborative Writing Activity

1. Students form groups of three to five students.

2. Each student writes their own name and the names of everyone in their group at the top of their paper.

3. The class or group chooses a story genre.

4. Each student titles their paper with the selected genre.

5. Each student then writes one sentence, starting the story and establishing at least two elements of CROW.

6. When all students have completed their sentence, ask them to pass their paper to the student next to them. Establish a simple order of passing.

7. *Reading and Writing Fluency:* When a student receives a new story, that student now reads from the beginning of the story, proceeds to add any elements of CROW that are missing and continues the story. The student continues to write until the teacher says "finish up your thoughts." At that point, give another 15–30 seconds for students to finish. Then the teacher says, "Pause where you are and switch." The students pass their story to the next student.

8. Allow enough time for all students to read the story passed to them. Students must then make contextual decisions as they add their ideas to the story. Repeat this step for about a total of 10 minutes.

9. Instead of having the students write for a time period and then be given a period of time to finish their thought, use a time limit and cut students off at any point, thus making the next student pick up in mid-sentence, as it is in the game. It works well when the students are already comfortable with the game and how it works.

10. Tell the students to "End the story." Each student then writes an ending to the story they have in front of them.

11. *End with Acknowledgment:* When the groups have finished ending their stories, students thank their group members, and retrieve the story they started.

12. Give students the opportunity to read the stories aloud or in silence.

13. *Scanning Skills:* Have students box all words or phrases that create CROW, circle words and phrases that support genre, and underline all words and phrases that form steps 2 and 3 of the three-step story structure. Students should be able to tell what the main idea of the story is when these terms are read aloud.

14. *Feedback:* Students and teacher discuss if topics of "Focus" were met. For each story that is read, ask whether or not each element of CROW was established, whether a conflict was presented and if it was resolved. The rubric can provide additional detail to the discussion and/or serve as a self, group, or teacher assessment.

15. *Acknowledgment:* Indicate the end of the activity with a simple, "Give yourselves a hand!" The teacher and all students positively acknowledge one anothers' efforts.

INDIVIDUAL STORY WRITING

DIRECTIONS:

1. Ask the students to choose a story genre.

2. Each student titles their paper with the genre they will be using.

3. Have students write their own story in the chosen genre. They should be encouraged to write for at least 10 minutes.

4. *Scanning Skills*: When students are done, they will pass their story to another student. The other student checks for CROW, conflict, resolution, and genre.

5. *Rewriting:* Each student rewrites his story with any necessary corrections (optional).

CONTENT AREA STORIES

With slight variations, Did You Hear the One About...? and Story-Story are easily adaptable to reflect subject specific content. Collaborative and/or individual writing activities allow the students more time in which to think how content can accurately and creatively be portrayed in stories.

DIRECTIONS:

Follow the directions as given in the Game Plans and Writing Activity Plans for Did You Hear the One About...? or Story-Story. Adapt these games to creating content area stories in the following ways:
- When using Did You Hear the One About...?, ask the students to offer an object relevant to the unit of study.

- *When using Story-Story,* replace the audience's offer of a genre/style with an offer of a "Where and When in Time." Story-Story is a good structure to help students write historical fiction that may be useful in not only in Language Arts or History class, but also in other classes that perhaps are examining historic periods when advances in math or science occurred.

It is recommended that historical characters are not made to be the central characters of the story. When historic characters are used as the central characters of the story, historical inaccuracies will most likely be created, and the goal is not to rewrite history but to create historical fiction. In addition, storytellers may begin to sequentially retell historical events or explain a unit of study. If that type of activity is desired it can be effectively accomplished using the Sequential Content Review format structured by the game Yes, And-Planning.

Examples:
Social Studies: Story-Story
Where and When in Time: Boston area, April 18, 1775
Individual Improv Writing

> Sarah and Jonathon were in love and to be married. Their wedding was planned for April 19, 1775. They met briefly the night before at Sarah's family farm to discuss some last-minute plans, when suddenly, they both heard shouting coming toward them. It was Paul Revere who was interrupting them. Sarah did not care that the "British were coming." She was busy, but Jonathan jumped up, grabbed his gun and rode toward Lexington. He was proud to be a minuteman. The fighting was close. The first shot sounded like a "shot heard around the world." Sarah could not sleep all night. Jonathon returned exhausted the next day. He had fought the British and helped hide the arms stored in Concord. A war had begun, but that would not stop their wedding. Sarah and Jonathan were married later that month but there would be many more times in the coming years when Jonathan would grab his gun to fight the British.

Science: *Did You Hear The One* About "the Stratus Cloud?"
Individual Writing

> Sam the Stratus Cloud floated with all the other Stratus Clouds in the sky. Although they were usually crowded together and looked like a blanket in the sky, Sam always found room to play. Sam loved to look at the lovely Earth below, but when she looked up she was all alone. She was lost. Sam couldn't see the other Stratus clouds anywhere, but then she saw some big, happy Cumulus clouds making big puffy shapes in the sky. She asked them if they had seen the Stratus clouds. They said that the Stratus clouds are often ahead of the Cumulonimbus clouds, so Sam went to ask the Cumulonimbus clouds. These clouds appeared dark and grumpy and rumbled with thunder when she came close. She even got hit with a hailstone. A wind saw Sam and knew she shouldn't be there and blew her back to where all the other Status clouds were. The End.

Math: Basic Story Structure
Individual Writing

Finding time to write narrative stories about math may seem a stretch; however, students are very familiar with word problems. Use improv's simple three-step story structure and let students write and solve their own math story problems in narrative form. It can serve as a review or warm-up at the beginning or end of class and takes no more than 5 to 10 minutes.

> *(1. Establish CROW)* Miss Maggie, the baker, was making 50 pies for the festival. She could make and bake 5 pies every hour. *(2. Create a problem.)* She was just placing the last pie on the cart when suddenly, the cart collapsed. Half of her pies were ruined. The festival was to start in 5 hours and she had promised to bring 50 pies. *(Solve it)* She still had 25 pies, but she needed 25 more in 5 hours. She started making and baking 5 pies

every hour. At the end of the 5 hours she had made 25 pies. She put those on the cart with the 25 pies she had saved from the crash. She wheeled her 50 pies to the festival where they sold out quickly. Miss Maggie, the baker, was happy.

Social Studies: Did You Hear the One About "the Shoelace?"
Where and When in time: America's Great Depression
Collaborative Writing

Student A:	Shelly the Shoelace was dusty from working in the fields of Oklahoma during the Dust Bowl.
Student B:	She was laced tightly up a boot and was beginning to fray. She worried she might break soon and saw the shoelace in the other boot laughing at her.
Student C:	Shelly knew her girl was too poor to replace her because they had lost all their crops. She knew she had to hold on as the girl and her family made their way to California.
Student D:	Shelly looked forward to California because she would walk through orange or strawberry groves and there would be no more dust.
Student E:	The Model A Ford truck the girl and her family drove broke down a lot.
Student F:	So Shelly had to hold herself together with all the walking the girl did.
Student G:	When everyone climbed on another truck Shelly and the mean shoelace realized that most other people did not even have shoes or boots.
Student H:	When they arrived in California they found work in an orange grove.
Student I:	But Shelly was about to break from exhaustion. Shelly began to panic when the girl got a new shoelace to replace her.
Teacher:	End it.
Student J:	But the girl washed Shelly and used her to tie her hair back. Shelly was happy. The End.

Science: Did You Hear The One About "the Microscope?"
Collaborative Writing

Student A:	Manny the Microscope sat on the lab table waiting for his new slides.
Student B:	He was so happy when they came that he accidentally fogged his favorite lens.
Student C:	Manny panicked. Everything was blurry. He couldn't see if it was an onion skin, or a hair, or DNA.
Student D:	He kept switching his objectives, but it just got blurrier.
Teacher:	End it.
Student F:	Suddenly, he felt lens paper over his lens. He could finally see his new slide of onion skin. He was very happy. The End.

7

ADDITIONAL GAMES:

For Integration into the Sequence

Although the Additional Games are optional, they can serve as powerful and fun tools in helping some students unleash their creativity and develop confidence. Students whose perceptual and kinesthetic skills are stronger than their verbal skills and/or whose bodies crave movement in order to focus (Hannaford 1995; Kranowitz 1998) may be better reached by these games, which are more movement and visually oriented. Those students who are visually-spatially or kinesthetically inclined will have the opportunity to acquire and apply the specified skills in a way that is natural for them, as well as an opportunity to excel in front of their classmates and teachers.

These games are separated from the Core Sequence because:

✓ The facilitator will need to feel comfortable directing movement-based activities.

✓ The students will need to develop some level of comfort moving in front of their peers.

✓ Some of the games create scenes and therefore require some basic staging and drama techniques.

ZIP-ZAP-ZOP

Although *Zip-Zap-Zop* is not a required core game, it should be used as soon as the teacher is comfortable leading it. *Zip-Zap-Zop* is a theater game and not an improv game as it is not framed with "Yes, and...". It is, however, extremely effective at helping develop basic communication skills. *Zip-Zap-Zop* serves as a highly effective warm-up and skill builder, and can easily be integrated into content-based lessons. The skills described in the *Zip-Zap-Zop* Game Plan develop gradually for most students. Through this game, it is possible to discover which students might be the extroverts, introverts, quick thinkers, or who freeze under pressure. *Zip-Zap-Zop* may also reveal students who lack physical coordination, are peripheral learners, or who may have auditory or speech difficulties.

* Serves as a warm-up.

* Helps build essential communication skills, verbal spontaneity, attention, and focus.

* Game structure can be used to review curricular content and for brainstorming.

* Can be introduced before #1 Yes, And-Planning.

GAME EXAMPLE

Students stand in a circle facing one another and pass the syllables, "Zip," "Zap," and "Zop" randomly around the circle. When passing a syllable, the student must make eye contact with the student they are passing to, turn their body toward them, and make a kind of pointing gesture and clapping noise as they pass the syllable. Although this is a game that requires movement, students do not move from their place in the circle when making the clapping/pointing gesture.

GAME PLAN

FOCUS: 1. Giving and Taking Attention 2. Communication Skills: speaking, listening, eye contact	GOALS/OBJECTIVES: See Rubric STUDENT POSITIONING: Standing in circle at desks or open space

DIRECTIONS:

Creating Relevance

Being heard and thinking quickly

Teacher:
A: Communication Skills

» Raise your hand if you've ever given a correct answer, but the teacher gives the credit to someone else who said it after you.

» Raise your hand if you've ever been out with your friends and someone says, "What do you want to do?" You come up with an idea, but your other friend gets credit for it when they say it?

» Have you ever gone up to the teacher's desk to ask them a question and the teacher doesn't even seem to notice you?

» Wouldn't it be awful, if you finally got the courage to ask someone to go see a movie and they walked away from you?

» Well it might not be because they are ignoring you. It might be because they just never heard what you were saying, or they didn't realize you were speaking to them.

» That is really unfortunate. If you actually make the effort to say something, don't you want to be heard? You want people to know you are talking to them. Right? Here is a game that can help everyone work on skills that will help them be heard.

B. Spontaneous Thinking Skills

» Did a teacher ever ask a question and you knew the answer, but when the teacher called on you, you went blank?

» That can feel embarrassing and be frustrating, can't it?

» Here is a game that can help you not go blank.

Introduce Game

1. *Demonstrate:* Follow steps 2–10. Teacher will demonstrate and participate with students.

2. Students stand in a circle.

3. One student begins by doing three actions simultaneously: a) The student says "Zip" loud enough for everyone to hear. b) The student makes eye contact with the person to whom they are passing "Zip." c) The student holds one hand out in front of them, like a handshake. Then the student slides the other hand by it to make a 'Clap.' The other hand, which just created the clapping sound, extends it as if pointing at the receiving student, but is not pointing with fingers.

4. The receiving student then passes "Zap" to another student, using the same simultaneous actions described in 3b and 3c.

5. The next receiving student then passes "Zop" to another student, using the same simultaneous actions described in 3b and 3c.

6. The game continues in this way with students passing "Zip-Zap-Zop", first sequentially around the circle and then randomly.

7. Encourage the students to increase the speed with which they pass each syllable.

8. Encourage the students to pass Zip-Zap-Zop properly for a set length of time, for example 15 seconds. This challenge can be fun and keeps them engaged. Students are competing against the clock and not one another; therefore students are not eliminated and can develop essential communication skills.

9. *End with Acknowledgment:* The teacher can indicate the end of the game with a simple, "Give yourselves a hand!" The teacher and all students positively acknowledge one anothers' efforts.

Practice

10. Practice steps 2–12.

11. *Feedback:* Students and teacher discuss if topics of "Focus" were achieved. "Was it clear when someone was passing to you?" "Were the passes loud enough?" "Was eye contact being made?" The rubric can provide additional detail to the discussion and/or serve as a self, group, or teacher assessment.

Apply

12. *Transference:* See "Adaptations and Integrations" for ideas on how to use Zip-Zap-Zop to structure content review and brainstorming sessions. Desired skills will continue to develop while content is reinforced.

COACHING & NOTES

TEACHER'S NOTES:

✓ **Warm-up/Energizer** Zip-Zap-Zop serves as a daily warm-up or energizer. This game is not an icebreaker to be used once or twice. The skills listed under Objective/Goals, and in the corresponding rubric, develop gradually. Zip-Zap-Zop develops individual communication and interpersonal skills. If its daily use in this form is difficult to justify, integrate content so it serves as a review of content material. Examples are in the following "Adaptations and Integrations" section.

✓ **Least Threatening** This game is noncompetitive. Refrain from eliminating students if they make a mistake. The warm-up is about developing skills. Students often suggest calling others "out," to make it competitive and more "fun." An effective means of making this competitive is to compete against the clock.

Ask students to keep the Zip-Zap-Zop pass going for a set amount of time, for instance 10 seconds, then increase it to 20 seconds, then 30 seconds and so on.

✓ **Identifying Challenges** This game can help teachers quickly identify challenges students may face in a learning environment. Students should still be encouraged to participate in this game to the best of their ability.

> **Hearing and Speech** If hearing or articulating the difference between "Zip, Zap, and Zop" appears to be too difficult for the students, then use something like, "1, 2, and 3."

> **Movement** Individuals who have impaired movement may still be able to participate in this game successfully. This game is about directing one's energy toward another for the purpose of communicating. Even without the full physical gesture, a person using only eye contact or slight head movement may be able to pass the word.

> During a workshop, I observed a high school student who was confined to a wheel chair with spasmodic cerebral palsy playing Zip-Zap-Zop. He did not appear to be able to move much and did not seem to speak much either, but when someone passed "Zip" to him he mustered all of his energy and ability and passed "Zap" to the next student. He was only able to move his head slightly in the direction of the person he was passing to and he could not articulate "Zap" very well, but he was able to communicate clearly enough for the other students to receive and continue the pass. Like his classmates, he was able to repeatedly practice important communication and interpersonal skills during the game.

> **Peripheral Learners** Zip-Zap-Zop is very effective in revealing individuals who may be peripheral learners. These individuals may appear to be disinterested and disengaged because of their consistent lack of eye contact, body language, and posture when instruction or dialogue is occurring. Zip-Zap-Zop exposes their ability to be aware and engaged. Although they respond immediately, they should still be encouraged to make eye contact and direct their energy when passing to a classmate.

ADAPTATIONS & INTEGRATIONS

RANDOM CONTENT REVIEW

Start the session with the *Zip-Zap-Zop* circle. Instead of saying, "Zip, Zap, or Zop," students say a random term from their homework, previous class, or unit of study. They will still use the actions described in step three of the Directions as they pass the term to another student. It's an energizing way to begin class and a quick means of assessing retention. Integrating Zip-Zap-Zop with content will help students continue to develop essential communication and spontaneous thinking skills. Students may freeze when passed to, so allow them to repeat terms already used from a previous student. This helps keep the students focused, the momentum going, and not stress the students as they develop the skills involved. By allowing the repeating of information from previous offers, the students' focus and attention will be stronger, and cries of "I already said that," will not disrupt the activity.

Examples:

English/Language Arts Romeo and Juliet Review	Science/Chemistry: Periodic Table Review
Student A: Romeo	Student A: O
Student E: Juliet	Student E: NA
Student A: poison	Student A: O (repeated)
Student G: Capulet	Student G: H
Student D: Romeo (repeated)	Student D: CL
Student M: balcony	Student M: I
Student L: swords	Student L: H (repeated)

BALL-TOSS VARIATION

The Zip-Zap-Zop circle is basically a ball-toss set-up without a ball. Set this review activity up as the Random Content Review but with a "catch." In a "catch-and-toss" format students do the movements as if they were catching and tossing an imaginary ball. For example, Student A offers or tosses an element from the Periodic Table. Student D defines it as they catch it, then tosses an abbreviation of a different element to another student. The throwing and catching movement helps focus and engage those students who crave and benefit from movement. Unlike in the random review, allow students who freeze or do not know the answer to repeat and pass what had been said the preceding turn. This keeps the momentum going and coverage of content progressing.

Examples:

Science/Chemistry: Periodic Table Review	Math: Computation	Social Studies: States and Capitals
Student A: AG	Student A: 2+2	Student A: California
Student D: Silver...CL	Student D: 4...+6	Student B: Sacramento...Alaska
Student E: Chlorine...NA	Student E: 10...-15	Student F: Juneau... Missouri
Student M: NA (repeats and passes)	Student M: -15 (repeats and passes)	Student M: Jefferson City...Texas
Student A: Sodium...Au	Student A: -5...+20	Student D: Texas (repeats and passes)

YES, AND-FLOW

Yes and-Flow encourages students to accept and build off one anothers' ideas through the use of visual observation and movement. Instead of saying "Yes, and...," students think and practice "Yes, and..." as they stand in a circle facing one another. One student begins a simple movement and all students mimic that movement until another student adds to the movement to create a new movement.

* Develops an understanding of "Yes, and..." through movement.

* Reinforces the notion that new ideas can come from building on existing ideas.

* Develops the skill of giving and taking attention through observation and movement.

* Can be introduced after #1 Yes, And-Planning.

GAME EXAMPLE

The class stands in a circle. There is no speaking, only observation and movement.

1. One students starts tapping their foot. The entire class mimics that movement.

2. Another student takes the attention and *adds* snapping their fingers. The entire class mimics the new movement.

3. Another student takes the attention and *adds* swaying their body back and forth. The class mimics this new movement.

4. Another student *adds* waving hands above head, but stops tapping feet. Class mimics new movement.

5. Another student *adds* smiling. Class mimics new movement.

GAME PLAN

FOCUS: 1. Giving and Taking Attention 2. "Yes, and..."	GOALS/OBJECTIVES: See Rubric MATERIALS: None or portable stereo STUDENT POSITIONING: Large open space in classroom Standing in circle around desks, but with room to move in place

DIRECTIONS:

Creating Relevance

New ideas are often created by adding to an existing idea.

Relevance can be created by helping students realize that they do not have to create ideas from scratch. They can create a new idea by building from an existing idea. Below is a guided question framework that helps students realize that new ideas are built on existing ideas, often only with a minor change.

» Did you ever feel really stuck when you had to come up with idea for a school project or an essay?

» Were you ever in a class or a group where everyone was sharing ideas and you felt like you had to come up with an idea that was completely different from everyone else's?

» Many of greatest ideas were created by people building on other ideas that already existed.

» Here is a game that can help you realize how to create new ideas by simply adding to or changing existing ones.

Introduce Game

1. *Demonstrate:* Follow steps 2–9. Teacher demonstrates and participates with students.

2. One student starts an activity (motion). The entire circle does the same activity.

3. After that activity has been established for a short time, another student takes the attention and adds to the activity slightly. The entire circle then copies that movement.

4. Keep repeating step 3 until all students have had a chance to alter the motion. The original move will disappear after a few turns as additional movements are incrementally added. Allow students to practice taking the attention before implementing step 5.

5. If some students do not take the attention, then after most students have participated, stop the activity. Start again, but have each student go in order of how they are standing until all students have had a turn.

6. This activity can be done with or without music. Try to initially implement this activity without music. Some students shy away from what they will perceive to be "dancing," and others will actually make the movements into complicated dance moves. If students seem hesitant without music then add it, but stress the use of simple movements.

7. Motions should be very simple and should flow or morph from one movement to the next.

8. *Acknowledgment:* The teacher can indicate the end of the game with a simple, "Give them a hand!" The teacher and all students positively acknowledge one another's efforts.

Practice

9. Repeat steps 2–11.

10. *Feedback:* Students and teacher discuss if topics of "Focus" were achieved. "Was attention being given?" "How could we better give attention?" "How could attention be more clearly taken?" The rubric can provide additional detail to the discussion and/or serve as a self, group, or teacher assessment.

COACHING & NOTES

TEACHER'S NOTES:

✓ Movements can be very simple such as tapping feet, snapping fingers, etc. For some students who become very restrained during this game, feel free to accept movements like smiling or even blinking. This keeps that student involved, as well as reinforcing the notion that new ideas can be created by one or more small changes.

✓ Do not initially add music. Many students may be excluded if music is added before students have mastered the concept of "Yes, and..." through movement. When music is added, students who can dance may create dance moves too complicated for others to imitate. For students who cannot imitate such moves, they will not be able to make an offer and are thus excluded.

✓ Add music after "Yes, and..." is mastered. Music can be fun and energizing. Remind students to start with a simple move. The class then continues to build off that move.

✓ "Denial" can still occur in this game if a student does not build off a movement, but changes it entirely in one offer.

FREEZE FRAME

Freeze Frame favors the more visual students who are sometimes less quick with verbal responses. This game may help engage those students in the other core games. Although this game requires movement, each scene begins with a repetitive movement done in place. There will be free movement as the scene develops between two students. Since the scene is complete in no more than four lines of dialogue, movement should be somewhat limited. Mapping out a small stage area will help contain the students' movement.

 ✳ Establishes story elements (CROW) while creating a scene.

 ✳ Requires minimal movement, basic staging, and acting skills.

 ✳ Can be introduced after #2 *We Are* or #4 *Volley Word*.

GAME EXAMPLE

Freeze Frame is a scene-based improv format involving two students. The primary student begins a simple motion. Another student joins the primary student, and offers one or more elements of CROW to start a scene. The primary student continues the scene offering needed CROW. Once CROW is established, the teacher says "Freeze." The student who joined the scene returns to the audience. The entire scene should be no more than three or four lines of dialogue, at most. The primary student returns to their initial repetitive movement and continues to do it until another student voluntarily joins them to establish an entirely different set of CROW. When CROW has been established, that student returns to the audience and the primary student returns to their original repetitive movement. A different student now joins the scene and establishes an entirely different set of CROW.

FRAME 1:
1. Student A does a *repetitive motion. (two hands in fists, with one on top of the other, in front of their body, being moved in a circular pattern)*
2. Student B: *(joins the scene)* Eye of newt and nose of frog, the princess will never break this spell.
3. Student A: Casting the spell from our cottage is so convenient.
4. Teacher: **Freeze!**
5. Audience:
 C: Two witches
 R: Friends
 O: To cast a spell on the Princess
 W: In a cottage
 * Future students <u>cannot</u> justify the motion as *stirring* with both hands.
END

FRAME 2:

1. Student A repeats the same *repetitive motion* done in Frame 1 *(two hands in fists, with one on top of the other, in front of their body, being moved in a circular pattern).*
2. Student D: *(joins the scene)* Dad, you're embarrassing me. That dance is so old and corny.
3. Student A: Chaperoning your school dance is just so much fun. I just can't help myself.
4. Teacher: **Freeze!**
5. Audience:

    C: Father and son

    R: Parent and child

    O: To dance and to stop the dancing

    W: At a school dance

    *Future students <u>cannot</u> justify the motion as *dancing*.

END

FRAME 3:

1. Student A does the same *repetitive motion* as in Frames 1 and 2.
2. Student E: That's strike two. One more and you're out of here.
3. Student A: Ha! This next pitch is out of here and we will win the World Series!
4. Teacher: **Freeze!**
5. Audience:

    C: Catcher and hitter

    R: Rivals

    O: To win the game

    W: At the World Series

    * Future students <u>cannot</u> justify the motion as *hitting*.

END

NEW TERMS & TOPICS

ASKING QUESTIONS

Asking questions during improv games fails to contribute necessary information to a developing scene. Questions waste opportunities to establish elements of CROW and to keep a story moving forward with action.

Questions Delay CROW

Dialogue	Elements of CROW
Student A: Sir Richard, hold my horse while I climb this ladder.	Character: Two knights Relationship: Friends Objective: To climb

Student B: Where are we?	No CROW offered.
Student C: We are at the tower where the princess is being held.	Where: Tower

Student A began to set up CROW. Student B's question delayed the scene from moving forward because it did not contribute any CROW. CROW could have been established quickly in two lines of dialogue as seen in the following example.

Dialogue	**Elements of CROW**
Student A: Sir Richard, hold my horse while I climb this ladder.	Character: Two knights Relationship: Friends Objective: To climb
Student B: I wish you could fall in love with a princess who wasn't a prisoner in a tower.	Where: Tower Objective: Further defined: To rescue princess

Questions Delay a Story from Moving Forward:

Audience Offer:	An archaeologist and a mummy at the North Pole
Student A:	Hand me the shovel. *(Student B hands Student A an imaginary shovel.)*
Student B:	Did you find something?
Student A:	I see a sleigh buried in the ice.

Instead the dialogue could have readily moved the scene forward as in the example below.

Audience Offer:	An archaeologist and a mummy at the North Pole.
Student A:	Hand me the shovel. *(Student B hands Student A an imaginary shovel.)*
Student B:	I see a sleigh buried in the ice.

BASIC STAGING

The following basic staging techniques should be introduced *before* playing Freeze Frame. Freeze Tag will also require an awareness of basic staging.

Upstaging

An actor "upstages" other actors by walking up stage, away from the audience. This forces the other actors to turn away from the audience in order to continue giving attention to the upstage actor. The audience has full view of the upstage actor's performance, while the other actors have mostly turned their backs to the audience, making their performance difficult if not impossible to view or hear. Many students will move up stage with no awareness of their location and how it impacts others. Simply ask them to move down stage or to the front part of the stage near the audience.

Cheating

"Cheating" is a simple direction for the actor to turn their face and body toward the audience without turning their whole body. It is to avoid offering the audience only a profile or the back of one's head or body. The "cheat" should look like a natural position. It will allow the audience to more fully view and subsequently hear the actor's performance. "Cheating" may be necessary when an actor is engaged with another actor or object that is up stage of them or even with them.

Opening to the Audience

This direction reminds the actor to "open" their body toward the audience so their performance can be better viewed. It is like a "cheat," but serves more as a reminder to not commit actions that would close off the view of one's body to the audience. For example, if one actor is falling off a cliff, the other actor should reach for them with their upstage hand. If they are reaching with their downstage hand they close off the view of their body and face from the audience. Although the actor will be able to see the actor's offer, the audience might not. It will be unclear to the audience what the next offer is based upon, and consequently not make sense to the audience. This direction will feel unnatural in the beginning, but much like cheating, will become more instinctive with experience.

ENDOWMENT

Although students may be familiar with accepting one anothers' offers during narrative storytelling, it is during the games of Freeze Frame and Freeze Tag that students will begin to give offers that will directly endow other's characters with qualities or talents. A student may tag into the scene and endow the other student as a police officer or superhero. One student may endow the other student with an emotional quality of being sad or a physical characteristic like being voraciously hungry or having long hair.

> ### *Example 1:*
> Student A: *(raises hand in the air and addresses Student B)* My dog ate my homework.
> Student B: *(takes posture and voice representative of a teacher)* Take this letter home to your parents.
> *Student A endowed Student B with the <u>character of a teacher</u>.*
>
> ### *Example 2:*
> Student A: *(With a sympathetic face)* Here, have a tissue.
> Student B: *(sniffling/crying)* I lost my puppy.
> *Student A endowed Student B with the <u>emotion of sadness</u>.*

Example 3

Student A:	*(With voice and posture of exasperation)* That's the third glass you've crushed in your hands tonight.
Student B:	Yeah, ever since I became a superhero, I just don't know my own strength. *(takes superhero-like stance)*

Student A endowed student B with the <u>physical trait of strength</u>.

GAME PLAN

FOCUS:	GOALS/OBJECTIVES: See Rubric
1. "Yes, and…"	
2. Giving and Taking Attention	**STUDENT POSITIONING:**
3. Establishing CROW	Open space in front of class

DIRECTIONS:

Introduce the Game

1. *Demonstrate:* A volunteer, Student A, stands in front of the class.

2. *Audience Offer:* Teacher asks class for an offer of a "boring and repetitive" motion such as, swinging, stirring, climbing, painting, etc. The reason for giving the offer to the audience is to reduce the sense of pressure a student might feel and to avoid choosing a "boring and repetitive" motion that may not be appropriate or is too difficult to work with. It is, however, an option to allow a student to start the scene by simply beginning a "boring and repetitive" motion of their choice.

3. Student A, standing in front of the class, starts a simple, boring, and repetitive motion, repeating it over and over.

4. Student B volunteers and while participating in the scene, offers Student A at least two elements of CROW. If the audience offered the motion of stirring, Student B can begin to establish CROW with stirring as the action, but only for the first scene

5. Student A may only speak and join the scene when enough CROW is established for them to accurately participate. Student A then contributes other elements of CROW.

6. Student B now has one line to add any elements of CROW still remaining. The scene is done as soon as all elements of CROW are realized. It may be finished in one, two, or three lines of dialogue.

7. As soon as CROW is complete, the teacher says, "Freeze!" Both players stop the scene.

8. The teacher asks the audience to name each element of CROW established.

9. The student who joined the scene returns to the audience and Student A resumes the same repetitive motion.

10. Another student gets up and follows steps 2–7, but establishes a whole new set of CROW.

11. Student A continues offering the same action at the beginning of each scene, until all students have participated or ideas are adequately exhausted.

12. *Acknowledgment:* The teacher can indicate the end of the game with a simple "Give them a hand!" The teacher and all students positively acknowledge one anothers' efforts.

Practice

13. Ask a new student to be student A and repeat steps 2–12.

14. *Feedback:* Students and teacher discuss if topics of "Focus" were achieved. "Was CROW established in three lines?" The rubric can provide additional detail to the discussion and/or serve as a self, group, or teacher assessment.

COACHING & NOTES

TEACHER'S NOTES:

✓ Let students volunteer when they have an idea.

✓ This game favors students with strong perceptual and kinesthetic skills.

✓ Sometimes it helps the students if they get involved in the scene without an idea. Some students are stronger perceptually when they are within the scene and not externally viewing it.

✓ If the same students are consistently volunteering first, you may ask them to count to five before getting up to tag into the scene. Often this is enough time to allow other students who are not as strong visually to participate. Sometimes they require a little more time to get an idea.

✓ Denials: Remind them that fighting does not move a scene forward. Fighting is a form of denial.

✓ Remind students that "asking questions" does not move the scene forward. Students should always add something to the scene. "Asking questions" also places more responsibility on the other students in the game/activity.

✓ Staging: Remind students to "cheat," "open to the audience," and not "upstage."

FREEZE TAG

Freeze Frame should be practiced before *Freeze Tag*. *Freeze Tag* is a more complex game with both students engaged in free and interactive movement as they establish CROW through the creation of scenes. Like Freeze Frame, *Freeze Tag* favors the more visual students. Unlike the story-telling games, which require only that students speak loud enough to be heard, improv games that involve the creation of scenes, like *Freeze Tag*, will require both stage and acting skills.

✴ Establishes CROW while creating a scene.

✴ Requires basic staging techniques because of the freedom of movement.

✴ Basic acting skills are helpful.

✴ May be introduced into the sequence after #4 *Did You Hear the One About...?"*

GAME EXAMPLE

This game is played by two students who begin by standing in front of the class. The teacher asks the audience for an offer, which will be the "characters and where" of a scene. The two students begin the scene. While establishing the remaining elements of CROW and moving the scene forward, the two students must physically change their positions. The teacher will call, "Freeze," when they are in a different, interesting, and interactive physical position. At that point another student "tags" one of the students out, assumes the exiting student's physical position and facial expression. The new student begins an entirely different scene by offering new CROW. The remaining student will take the attention by making an offer with any elements of CROW still missing and move the scene forward.

For example, two students start a scene, establish CROW and as they are shaking hands, the Teacher says, "Freeze!" Those two students freeze in that position. Another student tags one of the frozen students out and assumes the same position and facial expression. The student, who just tagged in, must begin a whole new scene from that position, but they cannot be shaking hands. They could begin the scene by perhaps thumb wrestling, saving the other from falling off a tight rope, or dancing.

Example

Teacher: **Who** do you want these two people to be?

Audience: two ballerinas

Teacher: **Where** do you want the two ballerinas to be?

Audience: in the jungle

(Students begin to walk through the jungle, slashing through vegetation on their toes using ballet type movements.)

Student A: My tutu is getting ruined with all these trees and bushes.

Student B: It shouldn't be much longer to the ballet. Wait, I heard a noise.

Student A: A lion! Run!

Student B: I'll grab the vine. Hang on!

(Student B reaches upward and grabs the 'vine.' Student A hugs him from behind.)

Teacher: **Freeze!**

C: Two ballerinas
R: Friends
0: To get to the ballet
W: In a jungle

TAG: *Student C tags student B out and joins the scene. Student C must not use hanging or swinging to justify the position and start a new scene.*

Student C: You can't stop me. I'll be the first astronaut to put our flag in Mars!

(Student C justifies the position as pulling away. Student A lets go of Student C and walks around to face Student C.)

Student A: (grabbing the flag) "Then I'll be first with you!"

(Both students are now holding the 'flag' as if they are trying to stick it in the ground.)

Teacher: **Freeze!**

C: Two astronauts
R: Rivals
0: To plant the flag first
W: On Mars

TAG: *Student D tags Student A out and joins the scene. Student D must not use sticking in something to justify the position and start a new scene.*

Student D: The fire is across town! I'll slide down the pole first.

(Student D begins to slide down the fire pole.)

Student C: OK! Watch out!

(Both students crash to the floor.)

Teacher: **Freeze!**
C: Two firefighters
R: Coworkers
0: To get to the fire
W: In the firehouse

NEW TERMS & TOPICS

PHYSICAL CONTACT

Once while playing Freeze Tag with my improv troupe, I screamed in surprise and in pain. As I was sitting on the floor with my legs crossed, the other player had tagged in and endowed me as a "Christmas tree ornament." She then proceeded to try and hang me on the "Christmas tree" by pulling me up by my hair, which was tied in pony tail. Ouch!

Five Rules for Physical Contact During Improvised Scenes

1. All physical contact must be appropriate.

2. No physical contact around the head and neck.

3. Physical contact must be made gently and respectfully.

4. Students should always be in full control of their bodies. No one should be dragged, lifted, pulled, pushed, etc.

5. "Play" fighting or wrestling that involves physical contact is not permitted.

Physical Fighting/Wrestling

Students may try to pursue physical fighting as a way to change their physical position during the game of Freeze Tag. Fighting is a form of "denial" and should be avoided on that fact alone. It does not move a scene forward, but instead stagnates it.

Do not allow students to touch one another in a manner congruent with fighting or wrestling. Explain to them that all fights on TV, film, and stage are NEVER improvised, but carefully choreographed and repeatedly rehearsed. Explain to them that those professional actors are trained to make fight moves look realistic, when in fact people are actually not touching each other, or they are simulating moves that avoid fragile parts of the body. For instance, during any type of choking move, the neck is actually not touched. In a hair pull move, hair is never actually pulled. Most importantly, the person being attacked is in control of the moves and is the one that makes the action look "real."

Students may have seen some improvisers actually engage in improvised physical conflict. Some improv troupes or sketch comedy troupes will engage in physical fighting in slow motion. Do not attempt this either. It is not necessary and not worth the risk. Unless your students are seriously trained in stage combat and have strong movement skills, just avoid all improvised fighting or you could end up with a real one.

GAME PLAN

FOCUS:	
1. Giving and Taking Attention 2. "Yes, and..." 3. Establishing CROW 4. Moving Scene Forward with Action 5. Basic Staging	**GOALS/OBJECTIVES:** See Rubric **STUDENT POSITIONING:** Open space in front of class

DIRECTIONS:

Introduce Game

1. *Demonstrate:* Follow steps 2–12.

2. Two students are chosen or volunteer and stand in a clear space facing the audience.

3. *Audience Offer:* The class suggests the "characters" for both students. The class then offers "where" they are.

4. Those two students start a scene establishing CROW in the first three lines of dialogue.

5. Once CROW is established the students must "move the scene forward" by physically changing the scene. Creating a "problem" or obstacle to their objective accomplishes this.

6. When the students have significantly changed their physical positioning, the teacher says, "Freeze!" At that moment the students freeze in that position.

7. At this time another student gets up and tags one of the students out. The tagged student leaves the scene.

8. The new student must take the <u>exact</u> position and facial expression of the previous student.

9. This student now must justify the position both students are in and begin a whole new scene.

10. The other frozen student may not move or join in the scene until they understand a sufficient amount of CROW in order to accurately participate.

11. Keep playing until all students have tagged in.

12. *End with Acknowledgment:* The teacher can indicate the end of the game with a simple, "Give them a hand!" The teacher and all students positively acknowledge one anothers' efforts.

Practice

13. Practice the game with the class following steps 2–14.

14. *Feedback:* Students and teacher discuss if topics of "Focus" were achieved. "Was

CROW established in three lines?" The rubric can provide additional detail to the discussion and/or serve as a self, group, or teacher assessment.

COACHING & NOTES

TEACHER'S NOTES:

✓ To increase the difficulty of the game, accept two unrelated characters as the offer for "Who do you want these two people to be?" For example, instead of two ballerinas, accept a ballerina and a cowboy.

✓ This game favors students with strong spatial and visual skills.

✓ When looking for a good spot to say "Freeze!," please be aware that some positions may get giggles from the audience. If you say "Freeze" and the position ends up being giggle worthy, (PG13 or worse) simply say, "Please continue the scene." Then try to finder a safer point at which to freeze them.

✓ Denial: Remind students to "Yes, and...". Fighting and asking questions are common forms of denial in this game.

✓ Remind students that "asking questions" does not move the scene forward.

✓ Remind students to keep scene moving forward with action.

✓ Remind students of basic staging techniques.

PART 3

*

STUDENT NOTEBOOK WORKSHEETS

*

RUBRICS

STUDENT WORKSHEETS

The following worksheets support the *Student Notebook* activities. Although the use of individual notebooks is recommended, if notebooks are not available, these worksheets can be reproduced and given to the students as needed. Below is a chart that indicates in which games and on what pages *Student Notebook* activities are introduced.

Core Games:

Game	Notebook Activity/Worksheet	Page #
#1 Yes, and-Planning	-none-	
#2 We Are	#1 CROW, #2 Where's	85–86
#3 Volley Word	#3 Story Writing	91
#4 Did You Hear...	#4 Journal Writing	97
# 5 Story-Story	#5 Genres/Story Styles	104–105

Name: _____ Date:_____

#1) C.R.O.W.

CHARACTER:

_____

_____

_____

RELATIONSHIP:

_____

_____

_____

OBJECTIVE:

_____

_____

_____

WHERE:

_____

_____

_____

Name: _____ Date:_____

#2) WHERE

_____:

_____

_____

_____

_____:

_____

_____

_____

_____:

_____

_____

_____

_____:

_____

_____

_____

Name(s):_____ Date:_____

_____

_____

_____

#3) STORY WRITING

Game:

Title:

Story Style:

_____

_____

_____

_____

_____

_____

_____

_____

_____

_____

_____

_____

_____

Name: _____ Date:_____

YES, AND...

HEY, LET'S PLAN A PARTY!

YES, AND...WE COULD HAVE A CAKE!

YES, AND...THE CAKE COULD HAVE BLUE FROSTING!

#4) JOURNAL ENTRY

_____

_____

_____

_____

_____

_____

_____

_____

_____

_____

_____

_____

_____

_____

_____

_____

_____

Name: _____ Date: _____

#5) GENRES/STORY STYLES

_____:

C: _____

R: _____

O: _____

W: _____

Found in Where: _____

_____:

C: _____

R: _____

O: _____

W: _____

Found in Where: _____

_____:

C: _____

R: _____

O: _____

W: _____

Found in Where: _____

RUBRICS

As examined in *Chapter 4*, the use of rubrics during the feedback phase of the games can increase the motivation to learn by providing individuals with a sense of power or competency over their learning. As discussed in *Chapter 5*, the rubrics offer the topics in the "Focus" section of each Game Plan in greater detail. The rubrics are not intended to create summative numerical grades for performances, but instead help to define clear learning goals for all involved. They serve the teacher and the students as a visual tool to help them focus on basic improv rules and essential skills for each individual game. Both the teacher and students can see how the games are scaffolded, understand expectations, and monitor progress. The rubrics might be used as:

► self, peer, or teacher assessments to help students gain an awareness of their growth and proficiency level of specific skills, while also informing the teacher of such progress

► surveys for students to self-assess their comfort with skills

► pre- and post-assessment tools to track skill development

RUBRIC

Name: _____ Date: _____

Use this rubric with: Yes, And-Planning, Zip-Zap-Zop & Yes, And-Flow.

COMMUNICATION SKILLS & COLLABORATIVE LEARNING SKILLS

Makes appropriate eye contact when speaking	
Directs attention & focus to the person to whom they are speaking	
Appropriate posture or physical actions	
Appropriate vocal projection or intonation	
Listens actively	
Listens until the other person is finished speaking	
Gives attention to others in an appropriate manner	
Takes attention from others in an appropriate manner	
Builds upon ideas presented by others	
Presents ideas without a fear of rejection	

CONFIDENCE, CREATIVITY & FOCUS

Commits to ideas	
Exhibits flexible & creative thinking skills	
Exhibits spontaneous thinking skills	
Speaks extemporaneously	
Remains focused and engaged throughout activity	

FEEDBACK

Is able to explain criteria	
Offers constructive feedback in the evaluation of their own work	
Offers constructive feedback in the evaluation of the work of others	

SCORING

Demonstrates consistency and quality in performing the indicated skills	4
Shows consistency and growth in their performance	3
Demonstrates inconsistency in their participation and/or quality of performance	2
Made no attempt or a very limited attempt at participating in the activities as they are designed	1

RUBRIC

Name: _____ Date: _____

Use this rubric with: We Are, Freeze Frame, & Freeze Tag.

COMMUNICATION SKILLS & COLLABORATIVE LEARNING SKILLS

Makes appropriate eye contact when speaking.	
Directs attention & focus to the person to whom they are speaking.	
Appropriate posture or physical actions	
Appropriate vocal projection	
Listens actively	
Listens until the other person is finished speaking	
Builds upon ideas presented by others	
Presents ideas without a fear of rejection	

CONFIDENCE, CREATIVITY & FOCUS

Commits to ideas	
Exhibits flexible & creative thinking skills	
Exhibits spontaneous thinking skills	
Speaks extemporaneously	

FEEDBACK

Is able to explain criteria	
Offers constructive feedback in the evaluation of their own work	
Offers constructive feedback in the evaluation of the work of others	

STORY ELEMENTS

Establishes the character, relationship, objective (plot) & where (setting) of a story	
Moves a story/scene forward through the use of action	
*Uses conflict and resolution in storytelling	

SCORING

The student demonstrates consistency and quality in performing the indicated skills	4
The student shows consistency and growth in their performance	3
The student demonstrates inconsistency in their participation and/or quality of performance	2
The student has made no attempt or a very limited attempt at participating in the activities as they are designed	1

*Not relevant to Freeze Frame or Freeze Tag

RUBRIC

Name: _____ Date: _____

Use this rubric with: Volley Word, Did You Hear the One About & Story-Story.

COMMUNICATION SKILLS/COLLABORATIVE LEARNING SKILLS

Makes appropriate eye contact when speaking	
Directs attention & focus to the person to whom they are speaking	
Appropriate posture or physical actions	
Appropriate vocal projection	
Listens actively.	
Builds upon ideas presented by others	
Presents ideas without a fear of rejection	

CONFIDENCE

Commits to ideas.	
Exhibits flexible & creative thinking skills	
Exhibits spontaneous thinking skills	
Speaks extemporaneously	

FEEDBACK

Is able to explain criteria	
Offers constructive feedback in the evaluation of their own work	
Offers constructive feedback in the evaluation of the work of others	

STORY ELEMENTS

Establishes the character, relationship, objective (plot) & where (setting) of a story	
Demonstrates the above in writing samples	
Moves a story forward through the use of action	
Demonstrates the above in writing samples	
Uses conflict and resolution in storytelling	
Demonstrates the above in writing samples	
*Identifies and uses different genres in their storytelling and writing	
*Demonstrates the above in writing samples	

SCORING

The student demonstrates consistency and quality in performing the indicated skills.	4
The student demonstrates consistency and growth in their performance	3
The student demonstrates inconsistency in their participation and/or quality of performance	2
The students have made no attempt or a very limited attempt	1

*Not relevant for Volley Word. Optional for Did You Hear the One About...

REFERENCES

Allen, R. H. (2002). *Impact teaching-ideas and strategies for teachers to maximize student learning.* Boston, MA: Allyn & Bacon.

Allen, R. H. (2010). *High-impact teaching strategies for the 'xyz' era of education.* Boston, MA: Allyn & Bacon.

Anderman, L. & Leake, V. (2005). The ABCs of motivation: An alternative framework for teaching preservice teachers about motivation. *The Clearing House,* 78(5), 192-196.

Berk, R. A. & Trieber, R. H. (2009). Whose classroom is it anyway? Improvisation as a teaching tool. *Journal on Excellence in College Teaching,* 20(3), 29-60.

Bidwell, S. M. (1990). Using drama to increase motivation, comprehension, and fluency. *Journal of Reading,* 34 (1), 38-41.

Black, P., & Wiliam, D. (1998). Assessment and classroom learning. *Assessment in Education: Principles, Policy and Practice,* 5(1), 7–73.

Bloom, B. S. (1956). *Taxonomy of Educational Objectives, Handbook I: The Cognitive Domain.* New York: David McKay Co Inc.

Britton, J., Burgess, T., Martin, N., McLeod, A., and Rosen., H. (1975). The development of writing activities, Urbana, Illinois: *National Council of Teachers of English,* 11-18.

Caldwell, H. & Monroe, B. H. (1993, November-December 1). Drama and drawing for narrative writing in primary grades. *Journal of Educational Research,* 87(2), 100-110.

Campbell, E. (1998). Teaching strategies to foster deep versus surface learning. Ottawa, Canada: University of Ottawa, Center for University Teaching.(Available from www.uottawa.ca/academic/cut/options/Nov_98/TeachingStrategies.)

Cantor. (2003, April 28). Improvisation makes learning child's play. *Rutgers Focus.* Retrieved from http://urwebsrv.rutgers.edu/focus/article/Improvisation%20makes%20learning%20child%27s%20play/1115/

Common Core State Standards. (2010). *Common Core State Standards for English Language Arts & Literacy in History/ Social Studies, Science and Technical Subjects.* Retrieved June 1, 2011, from www.corestandards.org/assets-/CCSSI_ELA%Standards.pdf

DeMichele, M. (2015). Improv and ink: Increasing individual writing fluency with collaborative improv. *International Journal of Education and the Arts,* 16(10). Retrieved from http://www.ijea.org/v16n10/.

Entwistle, N. (2004, June). Teaching-learning environment to support deep learning in contrasting subject areas. Paper presented at StaffordshireUniversity, Stafford, UK.

Gardner, H. (1993). *Multiple intelligences: The theory in practice.* New York: Basic Books.

Gillard, M. (1996). *Storyteller, story teacher: Discovering the power of storytelling for teaching and living.* York, ME: Stenhouse.

Glasser, W. (1998). *Choice theory: A new psychology of personal freedom.* New York: Harper Collins Publishers.

Graham, S., & Perin, D. (2007).*Writing next: Effective strategies to improve writing of adolescents in middle and high schools –* A report to Carnegie Corporation of New York. Washington, D.C. Alliance for Excellent Education.

Hannaford, C. (1995). *Smart moves.* Arlington, VA: Great Ocean Publishing.

Jensen, E. (2001). *Arts with the brain in mind.* Alexandria, VA: Association for Supervision and Curriculum Development.

Jensen, E. (2005). *Teaching with the brain in mind.* (2nd ed.)Alexandria, VA: Association for Supervision and Curriculum Development.

Jensen, E. (2008). *Brain based learning: The new paradigm of teaching. (2nd ed.)* Thousand Oaks, CA: Corwin Press.

Kagan, S. (1994). *Cooperative learning. (2nd ed.)* San Clemente, CA: Kagan Cooperative Learning.

Krache, D. (2012, September, 17). *Nation's Report Card: Writing test shows gender gap.* Retrieved from http://schoolsofthought.blogs.cnn.com/2012/09/17/nations-report-card-writing-test-shows-gender-gap/

Krathwohl, D. R., Bloom, B. S., & Masia, B. B. (1964). *Taxonomy of educational objectives; the classification of educational goals. Handbook II: The affective domain.* New York: Longman, Green.

Kranowitz, C. S. (1998). *The out-of-sync-child.* New York, NY: Skylight Press.

Limb, C. (2010, November). *Your Brain on Improv* [Video file}. Retrieved from http://www.ted.com/talks/charles_limb_your_brain_on_improv.html

Lopez-Gonzalez M. & Limb, C. (2012). Musical Creativity and the Brain. Cerebrum. *The Dana Foundation.* Retrieved from http://dana.org/news/cerebrum/detail.aspx?id=35670

McCarthy, B & McCarthy D. (2006). *Teaching around the 4MAT cycle: Designing instruction for diverse learners & diverse learning.* Thousand Oaks, CA: Corwin Press.

McKnight, K. S. (2000). *Firing the canon: An examination of teaching methods for engaging high school student in canonical literature.* (Doctoral dissertation). Retrieved from http://indigo.uic.edu/handle/10027/17840.

McMaster, J. C. (1998). "Doing" literature: Using drama to build literacy. *The Reading Teacher,* 51(7), 574-584.

Medical improv training hones doctor-patient skills. (2013, July 17). National University of Health Sciences News Center. Retrieved from https://www.nuhs.edu/news/2013/7/medical-improv-training-hones-doctor-patient-skills/

Moffett, J. {1968} 1983. *Teaching the Universe of Discourse.* Boston: Houghton Mifflin.

Moffit, D. E. (n.d.) *Viola Spolin biography.* Spolin Center. Retrieved July 1, 2010, from www.spolin/violabio.html

National Center for Education Statistics (2012). *The Nation's Report Card: Writing 2011 (NCES 2012-470).* Institute of Education Sciences, U.S. Department of Education, Washington D.C.

Panitz, Ted. (1996). *A definition of collaborative v. cooperative learning.* Deliberation. Retrieved July 15, 2010, from www. london met.ac.uk/deliberations/collaborative-learning/panitz-paper.cfm

Podlozny, A. (2000). Strengthening verbal skills through the use of classroom drama: A clear link. *Journal of Aesthetic Education.* 34(3/4), 239-275.

Rhem, J. (1995). Deep/surface approaches to learning: An introduction. *The National Teaching and Learning Forum,* 5(1), 1-3.

Reichert, Michael & Richard Hawley. (2010). *Reaching boys teaching boys: Strategies that work and why.* San Francisco, CA: Jossey-Bass.

Sawyer, R.K. (2002). Improvisation and narrative. *Narrative Inquiry,* 12(2), 319-349.

Sawyer, R. K. (2003). *Improvised dialogues: Emergence and creativity in conversation.* Westport, CT: Greenwood Press.

Sawyer, R. K. (2004, March). Creative teaching: Collaborative discussion as disciplined improvisation. *Educational Research,* 33(2), 12-20.

Sawyer, R.K. (2004, June). Improvised lessons: Collaborative discussion in the constructionist classroom. *Teaching Education,* 15(2), 189-201. DOI: 10.1080/1047621042000213610

Sawyer, R. K. (2006). Educating for innovation: Thinking skills and creativity, 41-48.Retrieved from http://www.artsci.wustl.edu/~ksawyer/PDFs/Thinkjournal.pdf

Sawyer, R. K. (2007). *Group genius: The creative power of collaboration.* New York, NY: Basic Books.

Sawyer, R. K. (2011). *Structure and improvisation in creative teaching.* NY: Cambridge University Press.

Scinto, J. (2014, June 27). Why improv training is great business training. [Online forum article] Forbes Magazine. Retrieved from http://www.forbes.com/sites/forbesleadershipforum/2014/06/27/why-improv-training-is-great-business-training/

Simich-Dudgeon, C. (1998). Classroom strategies for encouraging collaborative Discussion: Directions in language and education. *National Clearinghouse for Bilingual Education,* 12, 2-15.

Smith, K. & McKnight, K. S. (2009). Remembering to laugh and explore: Improvisational Activities for literacy teaching in urban classrooms. *International Journal of Education & the Arts,* 10(12). Retrieved 6/23/2010 from http://www.ijea.org/v10n12/.

Sparks, Dennis. (1999, Spring) Assessment without victims: An interview with Rick Stiggins. *Journal of Staff Development,* 20,(2). Retrieved from www. Learning forward.org/news/jsd/stiggens202.cfm

Sousa, David A. (2011). *How the brain learns* (4th ed.) Thousand Oaks, CA: Corwin Press.

Spolin, V. quoted in *Los Angeles Times,* May 26, 1974.

Spolin, V. (1986). *Theater games for the classroom: A teacher's handbook.* Evanston, IL: Northwestern University Press.

Spolin, V. (1999). *Improvisation for the Theater* (3rd ed.). Evanston, IL: Northwestern University Press.

Spolin, V. (2011). *Theater games for rehearsal: A director's handbook updated edition.* Evanston, IL: Northwestern University Press.

Sullo, B. (2007). *Activating the desire to learn.* Alexandria, VA: Association for Supervision and Curriculum Development.

Stiggins, R. J. (2011). *Student-Involved Assessment FOR Learning (6th ed.).* New Jersey: Pearson Prentice Hall.

Stiggins, R. J. (2007, May). Assessment Through the Student's Eyes. *Educational Leadership,* 64(8), 22-26.

Unlock your negotiation potential with the art of improvisation. (2015). [Online catalogue] Retrieved from http://law.pepperdine.edu/straus/training-and-conferences/professional-skills-program-summer/improvisational-negotiation.htm

Vygotsky, L. S. 1978. *Mind in society: The development of higher psychological processes.* Cambridge, MA: Harvard University Press.

Wagner, B.J. (1998). *Educational drama and language arts: What research shows.* Portsmouth, MA: Heinemann.

Wilhelm, J. D. (1997). *You gotta be the book.* New York, NY: Teachers College Press.

Yaffe, S. H. (1989). Drama as a teaching tool. *Educational Leadership,* 46, (6), 29-32.

Yau, M. (1992). Drama: Its potential as a teaching and learning tool. *Scope,* 7 (1), March 1992. (Also, ERIC Document ED. 343 179).

INDEX

ABOUT THE AUTHOR

*

Mary DeMichele is an educator with over 20 years of experience as a certified teacher, actor, trainer and consultant. She has taught and advocated for students of economically, educationally, and ethnically diverse backgrounds throughout the United States. Founder and director of Academic Play, she introduces teachers and trainers to activities and concepts from the performing arts that can be integrated into their classroom and organizations to energize the learning experience and empower individuals with valuable presentation skills, necessary interpersonal skills and essential literacy skills. She began her career as a social studies teacher in an urban district in New Jersey where she taught for over 10 years. There she founded a performing arts program, teaching both drama and improv as well as integrating them with academic subjects. She has worked in inner city, suburban and rural districts, as a social studies teacher, special needs teacher and educational director for foster care youth. Mary holds a Bachelor of Arts from Rutgers University and a Master of Social Science from Syracuse University.